I0649974

HAVE A LIVELY FAITH

HAVE A LIVELY FAITH

by

JOHN HEUSS

Rector of Trinity Parish
New York City

MOREHOUSE-BARLOW CO.

NEW YORK

PRINTED IN THE UNITED STATES OF AMERICA
BY THE HADDON CRAFTSMEN, INC., SCRANTON, PA.

Contents

6

Preface

This book deals with the faith of an Episcopalian. It has been published in the hope that it will help others to have a lively faith. It is an attempt to describe some of the great beliefs by which the historic Church has lived from its earliest days. It will tell you why I believe them and what difference they make today.

First of all, what is my faith? Let me make it very clear! My faith is the faith of the historic Catholic Church.

In short, it is not something which I invented. It is the result not of one erring, lonely child of God feebly reaching out to explore the whole range of history's experience. It is a faith which is the result of the experience of thousands of human beings from before Abraham, Isaac, Jacob, and Joseph down to the present day. It is the faith Christ taught in the Gospels. It is the same faith which St. Paul and the early Church believed. It is the faith of the Fathers of the early Church—of Irenaeus, of Origen, of Athanasius, of St. John Chrysostom, of John Scotus Eriugena, of St. Francis of Assisi, of Lancelot Andrewes, of John Keble and of the present Archbishop of Canterbury. It is the faith of sinners and saints, of scholars and mystics, of humble peasants and catholic princes. It is the faith, in short, of two thousand years of Catholic Christianity unmodified, on the one side, by dubious Protestant individualism and, on the other, preserved from the equally dubious individualism of an infallible pope. It is the faith professed by the Eastern Orthodox Churches, by the old Catholic Churches of Europe, and by the Anglican Communion throughout the world.

Having thus located it, let me now define in brief its content.

The barest statement of its content stands for anyone to peruse in the Apostles', Nicene, and Athanasian Creeds. Here history possesses its clearest and briefest statement of the historic faith. If anyone wishes to examine the logic upon which the statements contained in the Creeds rest, he will seek it in the voluminous, nevertheless carefully collected literature of the Fathers of the first six centuries and the only truly Ecumenical Councils of the same period.

Can one briefly summarize the content of this faith? Here, at least, is an attempt to do it. At the center stands an unshakable conviction in God. He is one God, and He has created everything. He can be described by His attributes, among which are omniscience, omnipotence, and omnipresence. Moreover, He is holy, righteous, just, merciful, perfect in love, but He will always be obeyed. And since He cannot be less than the highest of His creation, namely personality, whatever else He is, He must be at least a person, not merely a force or an intelligence.

Moreover, He has an eternal purpose which is being worked out in His creation. This purpose gradually has revealed itself in history, pre-eminently in the revelation of the prophets of the Old Testament, and in the life of Jesus Christ. This purpose, briefly put, is the development of personalities like Himself, who willingly choose to love Him as He loves them. The means whereby such ability to love perfectly is attained is by learning the redemptive power of sacrifice and by receiving the grace of God's Holy Spirit through the Sacraments.

To reveal perfectly the substance of faith, God at one time in history entered into human life and became incarnate in the person of Jesus Christ. In the teaching of Jesus, and by the act of perfect sacrifice which He made upon the Cross, man has a clear-cut blueprint of the way to perfection. He also has certainty concerning his ultimate victory through the Resurrection of Christ from the dead. He thus possesses a knowledge of God in terms of the flesh, which he can understand.

Moreover, since God does nothing in a chaotic fashion, and has organized to the minutest detail all the rest of His creation, it is not sensible to assume that He would leave the most precious of His creations, namely mankind, to the doubtful fate which attends all disorganization. Therefore, He created a Church. To it, He gave definite powers and definite commandments. Moreover, He did not give some of these responsibilities or powers to all of His followers. Rather, He wisely safeguarded the unity and continuity of His society by giving certain authority to the Apostles and their successors, the Bishops.

Much could be said concerning the meaning of this Church. It is enough here to remark that it is considered not as a voluntary association of like-minded people, gathering its authority from the individuals who compose it, but rather it is considered the divine extension of Christ's body on earth, receiving its authority first from Him.

Now a word as to the Church's ultimate victory. At present God is supremely at work in the world through the life of this Church: in each generation changing individuals, who in turn contribute, each his share, to the slow, gradual, long-time change of the whole human race. The change is away from the motive of selfishness, toward the willingness to live in co-operation and sacrifice with all other men. The victory of the Church is not to be judged by what it has accomplished or failed to accomplish in the present. The victory of the Church will not be realized in man-made schemes for union of the nations, for collective security, or for stemming or hastening the rate of social change. God's victory is not to be identified with the social stability of any class, upper or lower, nor with the permanency of democracy, or the reputed efficiency of totalitarianism. His victory will not be accomplished today or tomorrow, but in the long evolution of men in a future far ahead of us. Then will come to fruition what may now exist only as a spark in the evolutionary process, by which God realizes His ends. To have furthered in any way the victory of His kingdom is salvation for the individual. To have hindered it is damnation.

That, briefly and with many omissions, is the content of my faith. Nothing is omitted which the historic Catholic Church has always believed. In it is room for such doctrines as the Virgin Birth, the Communion of Saints, the Resurrection of the Dead, the Reality of our Lord's Presence at the Sacrament of the Altar, the power of Apostolically ordained clergy to forgive sins. In short, it is the total historic Christian faith. It contains no addition of a later Romanism, and is not watered down by a still later Protestantism.

Why do I believe it? The answer is a simple one. It has two parts. First, when I was searching, as a young seeker after that which would give to my life greater assurance that I would live and count for something in the long history of the race, I discovered that no great work was ever accomplished in the history of the so-called liberal individualist who did not know exactly what he believed. I recognized early that four score years and ten, if a man came to them, is too short a time for the long religious history of the race to be recapitulated in my experience, or for

9

anything but confused opinions to be reached. I, therefore, determined to give my allegiance to an authoritative religion, to one which was not the result of historical accident or individualistic prejudice. Fortunately, such a religion exists in the historic Catholic Church. Its authority was the divine authority of its founder, Jesus Christ, safeguarded by the continuity and wisdom of the Apostles, tested over and over again by the cumulative experience of thousands of men living in twenty centuries.

And second, I believe in the total faith of the historic Catholic Church because I have found in the writings of its Fathers a rational, intelligent answer *to every conceivable question* that doubt can raise, or theology can answer. I have never yet heard or read a question which was new to the historic faith. And not only has faith provided an answer, but the answer has been based upon close and careful reasoning, deep enough to satisfy the most exacting intellect. The end result has been that, the more I become familiar with the content of the Church's faith, the more I am convinced that much agnosticism, and even liberalism, is neither of these things at all. Rather, these words are polite euphemisms for those people who have neither the wit, in the first place, to know that the historic faith already dealt with these problems, or the depth of intellect or scholarly patience, in the second place, to find out what the Church has already said on the subject.

Now we come to the final question: What difference does such a lively faith make?

I will presume that by that question is meant what difference does it make to me personally. I can answer with complete confidence. My allegiance to the faith of the historic Church ended once and for all the confusion as to why I am on this earth, what life is all about, and what I should live for. Whenever anyone arrives at that point in his thinking, the wellsprings of his energies are directed in a specific direction. He becomes an effective person, and for the first time in his life really knows what it means to be happy. This is the peace of God which passeth all understanding. This is the realization of the meaning of that abundant life which our Master said He came into the world that men might have.

In the midst of a chaotic world cataclysm, such as we are now living in, this faith leaves one hopeful and certain of the ultimate triumph of righteousness. When one believes that that for which he works and lives has within it the divine purpose of God, no temporal darkness can fill him with confusion and with fear. He is not afraid of what will happen to institutions or to himself. Both may come down in ruin before the forces of evil. Nevertheless, that for which the Church has stood, and stands today, will never die. What happens in my day or to me is a matter of no ultimate concern. My faith makes it possible for me, in the midst of the present darkness, not only to live with hope but to live also with cheer.

I submit to you that that is a faith worth having.

John Heuss

HAVE A LIVELY FAITH

I

GOD, THE FATHER

1. God Makes History

In some places the Gospels read like a mystery story. For instance, St. John's Gospel tells of a furtive visit to Jesus by a man named Nicodemus in the dead of night. It is remarkable how many great events in our Lord's life took place at night. He was born in a stable at night. Shepherds heard the angels sing about the Saviour's birth at night. The Wise Men saw His star at night. The first miracle that He wrought, at Cana in Galilee, occurred at night. He healed Peter's mother at night. The Last Supper took place at night. He agonized in Gethsemane at night. He was arrested at night. His trial before the Sanhedrin was hastily convened at night. After the Resurrection He appeared to His disciples at night.

All of this suggests a great truth about God: He works quietly, almost hiddenly, in the affairs of nations and of men. God never makes the headlines. He is too busy making history!

What do you suppose would have been the headline if the Imperial City of Rome had had a newspaper on the morning of December 25, A. D. 1? Something like this perhaps: "Roman Legions Wipe Out Cyprus Rebellion." Or "Northern Barbarians Send Truce Ambassadors to Caesar." Or maybe "Roman Citizen Murdered in North Africa." Sounds familiar, doesn't it? I doubt if the headlines then and the headlines now would differ very much. But the news on December 25, A. D. 1, was not in the headlines. It was in a stable in the little town of Bethlehem. God had entered human life with a sound no greater than a baby's cry. In one night God began the work that was to topple Caesar from his throne and create a new order of civilization.

Only a fool would claim that front-page news does not seem important. But we all need to remember something. God never holds a press conference. He plants a seed. He creates a child. He inspires a prophet. He enlightens a scientist. He strengthens a martyr. He encourages a saint. And without any fanfare He changes and rules the world. We who are Christians need to live above the sweaty clamor of the sensational stories daily hurled at us by news commentators.

We must remember that God works in a different dimension than does a teletype machine. His dimension is the silent grandeur of eternity. As Christian people, we must raise our sights, and cultivate an eternity point of view. We always should live in the afterglow of Ascension Day. Like as we believe our "Lord Jesus Christ to have ascended into the heavens, so we may also in heart and mind thither ascend, and with him continually dwell."

If this be true, we then learn that the primary duty of the Church is to cultivate holiness, a duty which needs to be pointed out to American Christians with special emphasis. We are activists in religion. It is a Western trait. There is considerable evidence that the Church in the United States knows that it needs to be the champion of equality and justice among men. Praise God that it is! Yet the righteous zeal of the Church quickly corrodes into political propaganda unless it is rooted and grounded in piety. The first goal of the Church is holiness. The second is social action. A worshipper who is penitent for his own sins is more acceptable before the throne of God than a cause-proud fighter for justice whose motivation is sometimes courage, more frequently pride, and too often bitter hate.

Not long ago, representatives of the Russian Orthodox Church visited the United States. They were here as the guests of the National Council of the Churches of Christ in the United States. Before that, a delegation of American Church leaders went to Moscow to meet with Russian Christians. In the Americans' report, they announced their conviction that the leaders of the Russian Orthodox Church were not the blind tools of Communism. But they criticized the Russian Church for placing its

18

only emphasis on preparing men for Heaven, and leaving all earthly concern for human welfare to the whims of the Soviet State. When the Church is at its best, it unites two things: first, holiness; and second, righteousness.

When Nicodemus visited Jesus at night, what did he come for? He came to get an answer to one question. He knew the answers to a lot of things. This was no ordinary man by any means. He was a Pharisee, which meant that he was highly educated. He was a ruler of the Jews, which meant that he was powerful and well-to-do. Yet he was a troubled man. Knowledge, position, and wealth had somehow failed to clear up the mystery of life. He wanted to know from Christ when the Kingdom of God would come.

He received an immediate answer. "Ye must be born again." The Christian Church is primarily a place where men see God's love. If they see it, they become new men. Hope, humility, courage, the power to forgive and to love are reborn in them. When that rebirth takes place, they are capable of creating a better world in which to live.

We have an old saying that "cleanliness is next to Godliness." Nicodemus learned that the world will be clean and decent after men have become godly.

It should be our prayer for every Christian parish, especially our own, that it first make people holy. True believers will provide the power to produce a better congregation, a finer neighborhood, a more decent city, a nation of equality and justice, and a world where peace can be achieved.

2. The Generosity of God

A big landowner needed workmen for his vineyard. At dawn he hired the first group. They agreed to work for a specified wage. At nine o'clock he hired a second group. Again at noon and at three o'clock he gave work to two more groups. One hour before quitting time he hired the last workmen.

When the day was over, he paid everybody the same wage he had agreed to give those who had worked all day. Then trouble started. Those who had been out in the fields since sunup were furious. "These last have wrought but one hour, and thou hast made them equal unto us, which have borne the burden and heat of the day." This story, in the twentieth chapter of St. Matthew's Gospel, seems unfair.

I suppose every Christian wonders why Jesus told this story. He told it precisely because it has enough of a whiplash in it to make people sit up and think. What did Christ intend to teach us?

First, the parable teaches that God is just as concerned about the least useful people as he is about those who are paragons of virtue. The dimensions of God's love cannot be shrunk to fit what seems reasonable to us. Perhaps it can be illustrated in this way: some outstanding citizen of New York walks out of church and goes home to dinner. All his adult life he has been an honest, hard-working man. He has raised a fine family. He has worked hard for his church. He has helped to build a hospital. He has aided many charities. He was decorated by the Government for service during the war. He certainly has "borne the burden and heat of the day." He has the well-deserved respect of many friends.

Over on the Bowery on the same day another man stands aimlessly in front of a cheap hotel. He is a derelict. He is seedy-looking and badly needs a shave. He amounts to nothing. He lives by handouts, and probably has been in jail.

Which of these two men do you think God loves the most? No matter what we think is right, Jesus teaches in this parable that God loves both of them the same.

By the same token, He loves all kinds of people. Some of them may seem to us to be little worthy of His love. He loves a refined young matron in Greenwich, Connecticut. And He loves an unrefined Bohemian character in Greenwich Village. He loves the Boston blue-blood, and He loves the King of Saudi Arabia. He loves the President of the D.A.R., and He loves our new Puerto

20

Rican neighbors. This does not imply that God likes what certain people do. Christ's parable plainly shows that the landowner did not like men to be idle in the marketplace. Nevertheless God loves every person, good or bad. He will deal with each more generously than he deserves.

This parable teaches a further truth. Think how much better it would have been if those who had been hired early had rejoiced at the good fortune of those who waited anxiously nearly all day without work. Now those who were hired at the eleventh hour would take home money and be able to feed their families. Why is it that so often we who are fortunate begrudge a portion of that same good fortune to others who are in need?

Do you remember the elder brother in the parable of the Prodigal Son? Was he pleased because his brother had returned safely home? No, he went into a tantrum because the father had forgivingly received a wastrel. The spectacle of selfish greed displayed by the elder son is not a pretty one. How different is the picture Jesus paints of heaven when He says, ". . . joy shall be in heaven over one sinner that repenteth, more than over ninety and nine just persons, which need no repentance" (Luke 15:7).

What does all this mean for us? It means many vital things. Only a few applications from life around us can be mentioned here. Those who have had the right to sit anywhere they wished on a bus would be acting more godlike if they rejoiced that Negroes in the South now are getting the chance to enjoy the same right. Those who have enjoyed freedom in America for many years should rejoice that refugees from many countries are seeking the same benefit. Those who possess financial security should welcome the fact that business leadership, the Government, and labor unions are trying hard to make life more secure for the masses of our people. The problems of our age are hard to solve in the right way. We shall not make them easier by starting with the wrong attitude.

The note which the parable of the laborers in the vineyard strikes is that of the generosity of God's love. May we strive to have a large measure of that same generosity in our own hearts.

3. Is God's Revelation Finished?

Jesus spoke these words in His farewell discourse to His disciples: "I have yet many things to say unto you, but ye cannot bear them now. Howbeit when he, the Spirit of truth, is come, he will guide you into all truth . . ." (John 16:12-13). These words clearly state that before the Ascension the apostles did not yet know everything about Christ and His Church. They had much to learn. The question is: "Did they or their followers finally learn everything about the Christian religion? If so, did revelation stop at some point since Whitsunday? Or has it happened in every age, and does it still go on today?"

We know that the Holy Ghost, who is the Spirit of Truth, came to the disciples on the Day of Pentecost. What does the Church believe about the activity of the Holy Ghost today? Do we know all there is to know about the Christian religion? Or is God still enlarging and reshaping our understanding of the Faith once delivered to the Saints? Is revelation finished?

To begin with, let me say that the *essential* beliefs of the Church have been received through God's revelation once and for all. These basic beliefs are called dogmas. Dogmas never change. All Christian dogma is contained in the Apostles' and Nicene Creeds. Anything which is not in these two Creeds is not a dogma of Christian belief.

There are eight basic dogmas listed in the Apostles' Creed. Let me rehearse them for you. The Creed affirms:

1. I believe in God.
2. I believe in Jesus.
3. I believe in the Holy Ghost.
4. I believe in the Holy Catholic Church.
5. I believe in the communion of saints.

6. I believe in the forgiveness of sins.

7. I believe in the resurrection of the body.

8. I believe in life everlasting.

In addition to these eight dogmas, the Apostles' Creed lists three facts about God and ten facts about Jesus Christ. These are part of the dogma about God and Jesus. You will instantly recall what they are.

God is a Father. God is Almighty. God is the Creator of all things.

The dogmatic facts about Jesus are: He is the only Son of God the Father. He was conceived by action of the Holy Ghost. He was born of the Virgin Mary. He suffered physical and mental pain. He was crucified. He died and He was buried. He rose from the dead on the third day. He ascended into heaven. He is enthroned beside the Father in glory. He will be judge of the quick and the dead.

Thus the Apostles' Creed contains twenty-one dogmatic statements. These twenty-one creedal statements are the only dogmas in the Christian faith. It is these twenty-one dogmas which the Holy Ghost has revealed to the Church. It is these twenty-one dogmas which neither the passage of time nor any amount of new knowledge—religious or scientific—can ever change. Strip Christianity of every other belief, and these twenty-one statements will remain the final bedrock of our theological conviction. To put it another way, no belief is essential to salvation which is not contained in the Apostles' Creed.

This creed was formulated very early in the life of the Church. While the apostles still lived, this creed was created by the early Church. So, as far as these dogmas of the Church are concerned, the Holy Ghost spoke once, and for all time, in the earliest days of the Christian era. It is accurate therefore to say that no amount of new revelation can add or detract anything from the twenty-one dogmas of the Church's belief which it has held from the very beginning.

This does not mean that the Holy Ghost has stopped speaking. Nor does this mean that divine revelation ended with the death of the twelve apostles. Every century since the apostolic days has brought new conditions and new problems to the Christian Church. Even when the apostles had firmly established the twenty-one dogmatic beliefs of the Creed, Christ's words continued to remain true: "I have yet many things to say unto you, but ye cannot bear them now."

Consequently, a tabulation of additional beliefs had gradually to be worked out with great care by the Fathers of the Apostolic Church. This tabulation of additional Christian thought made necessary by new conditions in the world is called Christian doctrine. Doctrine differs from dogma. Dogma never changes. Doctrine, under strictly limited conditions, is subject to later revision and change.

There are two kinds of doctrine. First, there are the doctrines painstakingly worked out by the six great Christian Councils centuries ago. The first of these great councils was held in A. D. 325 and it gathered at the town of Nicaea in Asia Minor. The last took place in Constantinople in A. D. 680. In these first six centuries there was only one, undivided Christian Church in the whole world. Because the Roman Church finally split off from the Eastern Church of Byzantium in the seventh century, and because the Reformation further split the Holy Catholic Church of Western Europe into the present Roman Catholic Church and numerous Protestant churches in the sixteenth century, it has never been possible since A. D. 680 for Christians to hold another truly ecumenical council binding upon the entire Christian world. The point to remember is that all doctrine agreed upon by the first six great Christian councils is the kind of doctrine which has the force of dogma. What the great councils decided cannot lightly be changed by any branch of the catholic and apostolic churches of the world. The Eastern Orthodox Church cannot change this ecumenical doctrine. The Roman Catholic Church has no right to add to it or alter it, although it has foolishly tried to do so. A case in point is the Roman Catholic dogma of the Infallability of the Pope. This is not an ancient ecumenical doctrine at all. It is pious opinion forced on Roman Catholics in 1870. And the Anglican Communion cannot change these doctrines either.

Let me give you an example. Holy Communion was the only

worship service known to the early Christian Church. The early Fathers knew from their experience that Christ was always present when the bread and wine of Holy Communion were blessed and consecrated. The Creeds do not mention Holy Communion or the Presence of Christ in the bread and wine. This does not imply that Jesus does not come to us in this way. His Real Presence in the consecrated bread and wine is a doctrine carefully worked out by the Fathers of the Church in the first Six Councils of Christianity. This may not be in the Creed. But it is an early doctrine of the Church which has the force of dogma. It was a religious experience which the Holy Ghost led the leaders of Catholic Christianity to understand. It was one of the many things that Jesus had yet to say to His followers, which in the early days they were not yet ready to bear.

The thing to remember is that doctrines agreed upon by the six great ecumenical councils cannot be lightly altered and they have the force and effect of dogma even if they are not part of the Christian Creeds.

There is also a second kind of doctrine. This is the doctrine worked out by theologians since the last great Christian Council in A. D. 680. All of this doctrine falls within the category of "speculative theology." It is speculative because the entire Christian Church has never been united enough to study and discuss as one great church a final definitive and universally accepted answer to some of its most important new problems.

That is why today in the majority of great Christian bodies there is a deep desire for Christian unity. The world badly needs some kind of new universal Christian ecumenical council. That is why the Pope invited the Eastern Orthodox Churches to send delegates to a conference to discuss common problems. That is why the Archbishop of Canterbury and the Presiding Bishop of the Episcopal Church went to visit the Pope. That is why the churches of Eastern Orthodoxy, Anglicanism, and Protestantism have formed the World Council of Churches. That is why great efforts will be made in the years immediately ahead to get Roman Catholics and the rest of Christianity talking to each other once again.

This will not be easy. There may not be any possibility of reuniting the great Christian churches in our time. Yet it is highly probable that the danger to Christianity posed by Communism, as well as other great pressures of the present day, will force most of organized Christianity to find a way to discuss common problems.

Meanwhile each Christian group will pursue its own speculative doctrine. Rome may go as far as to declare as a dogma the speculation that the Blessed Virgin is co-existent in the consecrated bread and wine of the Mass with Jesus Christ her beloved Son. Some Protestant churches may try to unite on the speculative doctrine widely held among such groups that Apostolic Succession is of no importance. Both are examples of speculative doctrine.

We can see then that revelation is not finished. God is still speaking to His Church. He speaks through the same Holy Spirit which from the beginning has guided the mind of the Christian Church. The problem today is that the Holy Ghost is trying to speak to a divided and broken Christian Church. Yet in spite of that, God is still revealing His Holy Will to men.

Among the many things God is trying to say, two doctrines seem to stand out above all others. First, God is trying to reveal to our generation a clear-cut doctrine of man. All of Christianity is struggling today with the question: "What is man?" Is he made in the image of God, or is he a thinking animal? Is he a free, responsible creature? Or is he the slave and puppet of the state? Are all men equal, or is it ordained that the masses shall serve the desires of an elite clique? Do all men have equal rights? If so, how do we end the exploitation of man by man?

By and large, the Christian churches officially agree quite well already on a universal doctrine of man. They will need to make this Christian doctrine known with utmost clarity in our generation if we are to win the struggle with Communism which has a brutal doctrine of man.

The second doctrine which our generation is struggling to understand is the doctrine of the Church. Obviously, each branch of a divided Christianity cannot be right about the nature and organization of the Christian Church today. There is a great body of truth in the Roman Catholic Church. There are also many desir-

26

able values in the major Protestant bodies. But the Church of the future must inevitably be a far greater thing than exists anywhere today. God is willing a "coming great Church" into existence. We may not be able to see the immediate fulfillment of this vital revelation. But if the divided Christian churches can trust each other enough to talk intelligently with each other, who knows what great miracle God can bring to pass? I firmly believe that, as the churches engage in this dialogue, the Holy Spirit will disclose a greater doctrine of the Church than any yet known.

So, let us not despair. Revelation is not finished! Revelation still goes on. There are undoubtedly many things Christ wishes to say to Christian people, but we cannot bear them now. It took seven hundred years for a united Christendom to understand most of its important beliefs. At no time was the struggle to create a true, orthodox belief easy. It is not easy today. But we can rejoice that we live in a period of history when God is speaking with a very loud voice indeed to all His faithful followers.

4. What About the Trinity?

In preparation for a discussion of the doctrine of the Holy Trinity, let us review a few of the great beliefs of the Christian religion.

First, our faith begins not by speculating about what God may be like. It begins by looking at history to see what He has done. God is known to us by His mighty acts. Therefore, the belief upon which all other Christian doctrine rests is a belief in revelation.

Second, let us think about God's creation. There are only three ways to interpret the universe which God has made:

A) We can describe it as a meaningless accident. But if it is, life can have no greater purpose than to get all you can for yourself and "to hell with anybody else." Our sense of decency tells us that this crude and cynical materialism cannot be true.

B) Let us examine the opposite idea which the pantheist holds. To him the universe is completely filled by God in every part, so that

All nature is but art, unknown to thee:
All chance, direction, which thou canst not see:
All discord, harmony not understood;
All partial evil, universal good.

Alexander Pope*

This definitely is more attractive, but the trouble is that it is too attractive. Its weakness lies in what it overlooks. Everything in life is not that rosy. Such an explanation of the universe might have been all right for beautifully upholstered eighteenth century ladies in lavender and old lace. But pantheism is hard to swallow in a world where the memory of Hitler and Stalin do not make for pretty dreams.

C) So we conclude that in the universe two things are real: God who created it, and the evil that spoiled it.

Third, we have to wrestle with the problem: "If God is good, what is He doing about evil?" The Christian believes that God became a man and had a showdown with evil upon the Cross. Jesus of Nazareth broke the power of evil by an absorbing love that was so strong it could not destroy the integrity of His life. This is called the doctrine of Atonement, and by this example of love we are to live.

Fourth, we face the question: "Was this man, Jesus of Nazareth, really God?" If God solved the problem of evil by living and dying as a man, how could such a thing be? The belief that God took upon Himself our flesh and blood is the doctrine of the Incarnation.

Now we are ready to tackle the hardest question of all in the Christian Faith: "If God became a man, what does this do to the idea that there is only one God?" How can God be both the Father in Heaven, the Son Jesus Christ, and the Holy Ghost? The answer to this question is the doctrine of the Trinity.

---

* *The World's Great Religious Poetry*, ed. by Caroline Miles Hill, The Macmillan Co., New York, 1946, p. 105.

As we start to think about this idea, try to avoid the thought that the doctrine of the Trinity is either too difficult to understand, or that it is not important to daily life. On the first assumption, it is true that a Trinitarian God is not so cozy an idea as a Unitarian God. But the second assumption is the result of just plain bad Christian education. The Trinity is so important to Christian living that, if you do not grasp its significance, you never will be able adequately to live the religion it describes.

Let us begin by getting a clear picture of the Trinitarian belief. First we shall consider a simple statement and then the official statement of the Church in the words of the Athanasian Creed.

Christians believe that there is only one God. But in this God there are three distinct Persons. They are God the Father, who made us; God the Son, Jesus Christ, who saved us from the effect of evil and who is present with us in Holy Communion; and God the Holy Ghost, who guides us and gives us spiritual strength.

Those few sentences provide a brief descripition of what Christians believe about the Trinity.

Every church member, however, ought to recognize the more explicit official statement. Here is what the Athanasian Creed says:

> . . . the Catholic Faith is this: That we worship One God in Trinity, and Trinity in Unity; Neither confounding the Persons: nor dividing the Substance. For there is One Person of the Father, another of the Son: and another of the Holy Ghost. But the Godhead of the Father, of the Son and of the Holy Ghost is all one: the Glory equal, the Majesty co-eternal. Such as the Father is, such is the Son; and such is the Holy Ghost . . . The Father is made of none: neither created nor begotten. The Son is of the Father alone: not made nor created but begotten. The Holy Ghost is of the Father and of the Son: neither made, nor created, nor begotten, but proceeding . . . And in this Trinity none is afore, or after other: none is greater, or less than another; but the whole three Persons are co-eternal together: and co-equal . . .

The Athanasian Creed should leave no doubt in anybody's mind as to what the exactness of the Christian belief is: There is one

God. In God are three Persons. No one of the Persons is greater than the other. You may say, "What a terrific test of the human imagination it is to try to picture such a situation!" But do not give up.

Let us see now why the Church came to hold such a belief in God. The unadorned fact of the matter is that the earliest Christians had a new set of experiences of God which could not be explained in any other way.

Many people think that Christianity began with the simple words of Jesus, and that later mischievous, hairsplitting theologians made up complicated doctrines for some strange reason.

Actually, Christianity began with a very complicated religious experience; and, in order to explain it simply, the first Christians had to break open some long-cherished, old-fashioned religious ideas, because these old ideas no longer fitted what experience taught them to be true.

That men should find it necessary to do some revolutionary thinking certainly should not surprise us today! Columbus broke up the old idea that the earth was flat when he sailed the Atlantic Ocean. Louis Pasteur broke up the old idea about the origin of disease when he developed the germ theory. Einstein smashed the Newtonian physics to pieces with his new theories of the structure of the universe and, in doing so, made possible the smashing of the atom.

So it was that the early Christians, out of the necessity of what they had experienced firsthand about God, had to smash up the limitations men had thought were inherent in monotheism. Their experience of the Trinity showed that, while monotheism was true, it was even more remarkable than men had realized.

Yes, Christian experience forced the development of the idea of the Trinity. You are probably saying, "What does he mean by Christian experience? If he would make that clear, then I could see the whole idea!"

In the book *The Faith of the Church*,** there is an excellent

_____
** *The Faith of the Church*, James A. Pike and W. Norman Pittenger, Seabury Press, New York, 1951.

description used. Picture to yourself a young Roman citizen who knew a few Christian friends. One of the things which struck him about them was that in some strange way they were remarkably changed. When he asked questions, they were more than eager to tell him about their new life. As a result, he decided to attend one of the meetings of the group to which they belonged. While he did not understand much of what was going on,—which they called worship,—it certainly was apparent that this group was dominated by an 'esprit de corps' such as he had never known. This powerful Spirit was doing remarkable things with these people. It gave them the courage to face torture. It made them share their possessions. There was a kindness and thoughtfulness about them he would not have believed possible anywhere. Thus, without knowing what it was, our Roman friend was beginning to have an experience of God the Holy Spirit.

As he found himself attracted time and again to the meetings of this Spirit-filled group, he began to learn about One called Jesus. He found that these people were what they were because of their faith in Jesus. The time arrived when that which Jesus had said and done became so important to him that he found his whole set of values and his conduct changed. Christ had, in fact, become the Lord of his life. Nor was this Christ a far-away name and example. In time he learned to feel His unseen Presence when the group worshipped and communed. Now he had an experience of God the Son.

As he learned more about Jesus, he also learned about the Father, who had sent His Son and who had created all things. For the first time in his life the abstract, far-away idea of God became personal, real, and powerful. By now he had an experience of God the Father.

Do you not now see what had happened to this young Roman? He had experienced God in three different ways. Each experience was valid and it was very real. He had a Trinitarian religion long before he had a Trinitarian theology to describe his experience.

Now, this young Roman was not alone. This threefold experience was the experience of the whole early Church. This was the experience of the twelve apostles. This threefold experience has always been the experience of Christians in every age; so it was inevitable that the Church would revise the old-fashioned Unitarian idea of God. The disciples and the Church experienced a new and wonderful life with Christ. He was so unique that they could not describe Him except to say, "This man was and is God." They lived and shared this remarkable new life by the power of the Holy Spirit, which had first appeared at Pentecost. All these experiences are one: the Christian experience which forced the development of the idea of the Trinity.

The upshot of all this was that the old-fashioned, limited, Jewish idea of monotheism had to be revised to include the new Trinitarian experience. Monotheism was not abandoned. It was seen to be more mysterious, more wonderful, than previously had been realized.

Most people today begin their thinking about God with a conviction about His unity. If they do, then the Trinity, as an idea, is a complicated mystery.

But this approach may be both historically and religiously wrong. Start, as the disciples of Christ started, with a clear understanding of your own experience. First, you are part of the Spirit-filled Church. Then, you come to know the Christ whom the Church holds before men. And finally, through Christ, you have the love and the forgiveness of the Father who made us. Then, since this experience is so clear-cut and understandable, it will not be the Trinity which will be mysterious to you, but it will be God's unity which you will reverence as a great and wonderful Mystery.

If you do this, you will easily understand that part of the collect for Trinity Sunday, which says, ". . . [we] acknowledge the glory of the eternal Trinity, and in the power of the Divine Majesty [we] worship the Unity . . ."

II
GOD, THE SON

5. The Pre-Existence of Christ

There is a Christian belief which is rarely discussed today. This belief is called "The pre-existence of Christ." It means that Christ had an existence before He lived on earth!

First of all, the New Testament proclaims that Christ existed before His Incarnation as a human being. In the eighth chapter of the fourth Gospel, part of which is the Gospel for Passion Sunday, Jesus is talking to a group of his Jewish followers. These were not the twelve disciples. Rather, they were part of a large following He had built up in Palestine. They believed that He was the long hoped for Messiah.

The Messiah foretold by the Prophets of the Old Testament was not generally regarded by the Jews of Jesus' day in anything like the terms of the Christian idea of Jesus as Messiah. To the Jew, the Messiah was to be a great human leader. He would be a mighty warrior, who would overthrow the nations which had oppressed the Jews for centuries. He would be a great earthly king, who would rule them with justice and wisdom. Like Moses and David, he would be their chief religious person. It was not the business of the Jewish Messiah to add one single new idea to the teachings of the Law of Moses. God had already revealed all truth to Israel. These Jews, to whom Jesus was speaking, took fierce pride in the fact that they were descendants of Abraham. They knew the Law and the Prophets. What they wanted in a Messiah was a successful political and military leader.

So when Jesus said to them, "If ye continue in my word, then are ye my disciples indeed; And ye shall know the truth, and the truth shall make you free" (John 8:31-2), naturally they were astonished, and their pride was hurt. "They answered him, We be Abraham's seed, and were never in bondage to any man: how sayest thou, Ye shall be made free?" (John 8:33). "Art thou greater than our father Abraham, which is dead? . . . whom makest thou thyself?" (John 8:53).

The reply that Christ gave to these men angered them completely. He said, "Your father Abraham rejoiced to see my day: and he saw it, and was glad" (John 8:56). The Jews could not believe their ears. Said they, "Thou art not yet fifty years old, and hast thou seen Abraham?" (John 8:57). Then came the great pronouncement of the pre-existence of Christ from the lips of Jesus: "Verily, verily, I say unto you, Before Abraham was, I am" (John 8:58).

This statement is only one of several from the lips of Christ which make the same claim. Listen to these words: "For I came down from heaven, not to do mine own will, but the will of him that sent me" (John 6:38). Recall what Jesus said to Nicodemus: "And no man hath ascended up to heaven, but he that came down from heaven, even the Son of man which is in heaven" (John 3:13).

This claim by Christ of pre-existence greatly disturbed pious Jews. St. John writes, "The Jews . . . murmured . . . and . . . said, Is not this Jesus, the son of Joseph, whose father and mother we know? how is it then that he saith, I came down from heaven?" (John 6:41-2). It even upset His closest friends. "Many therefore of his disciples, when they had heard this, said, This is an hard saying; who can hear it?" (John 6:60).

It did not make matters any easier on this occasion when Christ tried to convince them further. "When Jesus knew in himself that his disciples murmured at it, he said unto them, Doth this offend you? What . . . if ye shall see the Son of man ascend up where he was before?" (John 6:61-2).

The idea of a pre-existent Messiah alienated many Jews. We read that "From that time many of his disciples went back, and walked no more with him" (John 6:66). Nevertheless it became a firm belief of the first Christians. St. Paul wrote it into many of his epistles. In Philippians he said, ". . . Christ Jesus: Who, being in the form of God, thought it not robbery to be equal with God: But made himself of no reputation, and took upon him the form of a servant, and was made in the likeness of men" (Phil. 2:5-7). In Corinthians Paul wrote, ". . . that, though he [Christ] was rich, yet for your sakes he became poor . . ." (II Cor. 8:9).

So all through the New Testament you will find this remarkable new belief that the Messiah did not start to exist when Jesus was born at Bethlehem. The earliest Christians then believed that Christ was co-eternal with the Father.

Secondly, let us try to picture what the existence of Christ was like *before* He became a man. The easiest way to do this is to put out of our thinking for a moment everything that makes up our image of Christ as the man Jesus. Before the Incarnation, the Son of God did not have a human body. He was not a Jew. He had no human family. He had not yet experienced the joys and sorrows of the flesh. He had not walked and talked with men as a man. He had not suffered death upon a cross. He was not yet the saviour of mankind.

Well, if He was none of these familiar things, what then was He? He was a Divine Person!

As the eternal Son of God He was subordinate to the Father. He obeyed. But this obedience involved no inferiority of essence to the Father! What is more, He was a Person with two very special responsibilities. He was the Creator of all things! Whatever has existed in heaven and earth was made by the Son of God acting for His Father.

Nor did Christ's responsibility end with creation. He also caused all revelation. Whatever man has learned has come to him through the eternal Christ. From the moment, long ago, when a primitive caveman was stirred by humanity's earliest dim idea, until today, when scholars are unlocking bit by bit the mystery of the cosmos, Christ was and is the active Divine Agent who stimulates all human thought.

Wherever a breakthrough has occurred in any branch of learning,

37

it is Christ the Revealer who uses a particularly keen and responsive human mind to make it possible. Revelation is not confined to knowledge of God and to religious matters. However, to reveal God to man with absolute clarity, and to make known the final authoritative relationship that God wishes to have exist between Himself and men, Christ the Revealer of all truth found it necessary to enter human life and become a man Himself. It was for this special revelation that the Incarnation was necessary.

Nowhere is this described better than in the opening chapter of St. John's Gospel: "In the beginning was the Word." (To the early Christian, "the Word" meant the Divine Wisdom empowered to create and enlighten the universe.) Now notice how St. John goes on: "and the Word was with God, and the Word was God. The same was in the beginning with God. All things were made by him; and without him was not any thing made that was made" (John 1:1-3). "And the Word was made flesh, and dwelt among us . . . full of grace and truth" (John 1:14).

The Church has never tried to describe what the pre-existent Christ looked like. What it has done is to proclaim—in the Nicene Creed—its faith that Jesus was the incarnation of "the only-begotten Son of God; Begotten of his Father before all worlds, God of God, Light of Light, Very God of very God; Begotten, not made; Being of one substance with the Father; By whom all things were made."

The things to remember about the pre-existent Christ are: He is a Person; He creates all things; He reveals all the knowledge mankind has.

What does all this mean for us? It does one important thing for every Christian. It helps us to realize the greatness of Jesus Christ, our Lord. Most of the time we picture Jesus as a noble and loving human being. We see Him first as a beautiful baby in the stable of Bethlehem. We can imagine His home life as a boy in Nazareth. We are familiar with Him as a man who gathered disciples and told amazingly simple stories about difficult daily problems. We are deeply moved by His compassion for troubled people. We see how courageously He died upon a cross. It is only at rare moments, such

38

as at His birth when the angel choirs sang, "Peace on earth, good will toward men"; or when He rises from the dead on Easter Day; or when, on Ascension Day, He is taken up into heaven, that we get brief hints as to Who He really is!

If we can imagine the magnitude of Christ's powerful and glorious condition before His birth as Jesus, we shall more clearly realize the meaning of the comfortable words in the Holy Communion Service: "So God loved the world, that he gave his only-begotten Son, to the end that all that believe in him should not perish, but have everlasting life" (Prayer Book, p. 76).

6. The Virgin Birth of Jesus

Some of you may have read or heard recently that one of the bishops of the Church questioned the doctrine of the Virgin Birth of Jesus. There can be no question as to what the Church has always believed. Anybody who tries to read into the words of the Nicene Creed: "Jesus Christ . . . was incarnate by the Holy Ghost of the Virgin Mary" something less than the doctrine of the Virgin Birth is tampering with words and playing fast and loose with the history of the Christian Church. To explain away the creedal statement: "conceived by the Holy Ghost, Born of the Virgin Mary" is to contradict the long-standing Faith of the Church and to abuse the clarity of language.

Why does the Church today believe in the Virgin Birth? To begin with, because two of the four Gospels clearly say so. The other two take the Virgin Birth for granted. The two Gospels which definitely speak about it are those of St. Matthew and St. Luke.

St. Mark starts his Gospel with the baptism of Jesus as a grown man. But notice how Mark begins. His opening words are: "The beginning of the Gospel of Jesus Christ, the *Son* of God." And what about the most scholarly of all the Gospels, St. John's? Here is his statement. Christ was born "not of blood, nor of the will of the flesh, nor of the will of man, but of God" (John 1:13). The Gospels of Mark and John, then, take the Virgin Birth for granted.

But let us go back for a moment to Matthew and Luke. We must remember that Matthew got the story of Christ's birth from St. Joseph. Luke on the other hand, got his information from Mary, the mother of Jesus. The first, Matthew, is written from the viewpoint of a bewildered but loyal husband. The second, Luke, from an equally astonished but obedient lady engaged to be married.

Listen to them speak. Here is Joseph's version in Matthew, chapter one: "When as his mother Mary was espoused . . . before [we] came together, she was found with child of the Holy Ghost." (Think for a moment what a shock that must have been to Joseph!) Now continue Matthew's account: "Then Joseph her husband, being a just man, and not willing to make her a . . . example, was minded to put her away privily." (Isn't that just exactly what you would expect any just, but indignant husband to do?) Yet Joseph did not do that, and here he tells why: "But while he thought on these things, behold, the angel of the Lord appeared unto him . . . saying, Joseph, thou son of David, fear not to take unto thee Mary thy wife: for that which is conceived in her is of the Holy Ghost. And she shall bring forth a son, and thou shalt call his name JESUS."

We do not know much about Joseph. But we do know one admirable thing about him. He trusted God; he trusted Mary; and he was a very good foster father to our Lord. Surely that entitles him to our respect and veneration as a saint.

Now let me show you Mary's side of the story. It has quite a different accent, because it is the story of a mother. She knew what had happened. Indeed, she was the only person in the world who really knew. And it was she who told it all to St. Luke, a physician:

> And the angel [Gabriel] came . . . and said, Hail thou that art highly favoured, the Lord is with thee: blessed art thou among women. And when she saw him, she was troubled at his saying, and cast in her mind what manner of salutation this

should be. And the angel said . . . Fear not, Mary: for thou hast found favour with God. And, behold, thou shalt conceive . . . and bring forth a son, and shalt call his name JESUS. He shall be great, and shall be called the Son of the Highest: and the Lord God shall give unto him the throne of his [ancestor] David: And he shall reign over the house of Jacob for ever; and of his kingdom there shall be no end.

Then said Mary unto the angel, How shall this be, seeing I know not a man? And the angel answered . . . The Holy Ghost shall come upon thee, and the power of the Highest shall overshadow thee: therefore also that holy thing which shall be born of thee shall be called the Son of God.

(Luke 1:28-35)

Years ago an art critic named Symonds stood in the Sistine Chapel and looked at the great paintings on the walls and domed ceiling. He wrote, "Every single part of that immense composition down to the smallest detail is necessary to the effect of the whole." This is true of the Gospels also. Take out the account of the Virgin Birth and irreparable damage is done to the story of the life and works of Jesus of Nazareth.

In our present day, those who are skeptical of the Virgin Birth usually base their arguments against its reality on two things. Students of comparative religion like to remind us that the Virgin Birth idea is not original with Christianity. They point out that the old pagan religions often taught that when a hero was born, he was frequently claimed to have been born of a virgin. They find parallels in the ancient Roman, Greek, Babylonian, Egyptian, and Persian mythologies. Then they smile condescendingly and challenge us to deny it.

Why should we deny it? Let us freely admit the pagan stories. But let us point out something the skeptics usually forget. The Christian Church does not claim that Jesus was divine because of His Virgin Birth. We claim that He was divine because of the unassailable morality of His life and His works, and because of His Resurrection from the Dead. You cannot compare the gentleness of Jesus, nor His simplicity, nor His compassion for people, nor His unerring insight into human life, nor His noble dignity, nor His self-sacrificing death upon the Cross with the swaggering, ambitious, lecherous tyrants who populate mythology. These so-called parallels of the Virgin Birth, which come to light in any college course in comparative religion, are not parallels at all. Not one of them comes close to approaching the spiritual and moral tone which is at the heart of the life of Jesus Christ. So that argument will not hold water.

Then there is the second modern argument against the Virgin Birth. To many people it is devastating. It is the so-called "scientific objection." The claim is that a Virgin Birth is scientifically impossible. But a young scientist from the University of Chicago, in a discussion about the Virgin Birth, stood up and said to the group, "I am a research biochemist and I believe in the Virgin Birth of Jesus. A virgin birth is not scientifically impossible. I am at work on a project right now in which eighteen generations of chicken eggs have been hatched without fertilization. Every one of them is a virgin birth!"

Any member of the Church should have no hesitation in facing any eugenist or any other scientist and saying, "Just what evidence do you have how God should be born into the world? All that you know is how human babies are generally born. What do you know about how God, the infinite and eternal, shall become incarnate in human life?" Even Huxley, the eminent British scientist and skeptic, once said to Bishop Charles Gore, "If I believed, as you do, that Jesus Christ was sinless and rose from the dead, then I would expect a physical miracle of his birth to parallel the moral miracle of his life."

In Christ we have a unique, moral being. No Moslem sings, "Mohammed, lover of my soul." No Jew cries out to Moses, "I need thee every hour." Given a unique being, such as Christ our Saviour was, we need not be surprised to find that he has a unique beginning and a unique ending.

Now this should be said. If a person cannot accept the Virgin Birth, he is not necessarily not a Christian. But, if a person does not believe in the Virgin Birth, pretty soon Jesus will become something less than God to him. People who stumble at the Virgin Birth soon stumble at the divinity of Christ. Those who stumble at His divinity soon stumble at the Resurrection. If they stumble at the Resurrection, it is not long before they no longer can believe in life after death. At this point, human life becomes at best heroic stoicism, or at worst a place where dog eats dog. The *whole* doctrine of Christ not only makes sense, but is man's one hope for a better world.

Let us rejoice and give thanks for the Christ who was born at Christmastide in the stable at Bethlehem. Let us also remember that it is not the Christ who was born over two thousand years ago who can save us. It is only the Christ who is reborn by faith in the heart of each one of us that can shine within us and irradiate the world. What the power of faith in Christ can do in our lives is the final proof that Jesus, whom the shepherds adored, is God.

We should want the whole Faith. Any version of it watered down by unfounded skepticism will never do. Therefore, believe in the Virgin Birth.

7. Did the Wise Men Come to Bethlehem?

In Epiphany the Church celebrates the coming of the Three Wise Men. Did such an event ever really take place? The answer is, "Yes!" The Church believes that the story of the coming of the Magi is true. There is ample evidence in addition to the account of it in the second chapter of St. Matthew's Gospel.

For example, the modern science of astronomy tells us that the "Star in the East," first described by the German scientist Kepler in 1604, not only occurred at the birth of Jesus, but appears regularly every 805 years. Its next appearance is scheduled for the year A. D. 2409. If you subtract backwards in history, it appeared in A. D. 799 and in 6 B. C. This last date is the one which is recognized by scholars as the year in which Christ was born.

It is known today that the Star of Bethlehem, this great and shining light in the winter heavens, is not really one star at all. Its size and brightness are caused by the conjunction of three planets. They are Jupiter, Saturn, and Mars. If one goes to the Hayden Planetarium in New York in the Christmas season, one will see an exhibit of the way in which these three stars appear to merge together to form one brilliant light. So one can be absolutely confident that the star, which the Gospels say hung over Bethlehem when Jesus was born, was there!

The second question is: "What about the Wise Men?" Is it not highly probable that the story about them is merely an imaginative tale? Once again the Church says, "The visit of the Magi to the Infant Jesus actually took place."

The Wise Men were astrologers. At that particular period in ancient history, the astrologers were the most learned men of their day. Astrologers believed two principal things: one, that the star-studded sky revealed an orderliness in the movement of the heavens; two, that the movement and position of the stars influenced events on earth.

Certainly they were correct about their first belief. There is a predictable orderliness about the movement of the stars. Out of astrology has grown the science of astronomy. It would be difficult, of course, to try to defend the astrologers' second belief, namely, that the movement of the stars determines what will happen on earth. Yet, the existence of these beliefs among ancient astrologers explains why three of them came to Bethlehem when Christ was born.

In astrology the constellation of the stars Jupiter, Mars, and Saturn was called "Pisces" or, in English, "the Fish." Whenever Jupiter and Saturn appeared, it was such an unusual event that wise men of old—and there were many of them in the ancient world—took this to mean that some great event would soon take place on earth. Obviously, therefore, the conjunction of these great stars set all of the astrologers into a state of expectation.

Now consider further. It was also believed that when Jupiter and Saturn appeared to come together, a king was to be born. These two stars line up in the heavens much more frequently than Jupiter, Saturn, and Mars do. So, the conjunction of all three stars meant to the astrologers that a super-king was to be born. He would be one who in his greatness would rule, not only over one nation, but over *all* the peoples of the earth. He would bring peace and prosperity, and would bind all mankind into one brotherhood. No wonder some of the wealthier astrologers set out on a long journey to find the newborn king.

But how did all three happen to arrive in the city of Jerusalem? Consider this! The horoscopes of the ancient astrologers had the sign of Virgo next to the sign of Pisces, the Fish. What did Virgo mean? It signified a Virgin, holding a sheaf of wheat. And the sheaf of wheat stood for the city of Jerusalem. At least three of the wealthy astrologers, who could afford to travel a long distance to pay homage to the great newborn king, came to the conclusion that their horoscopes indicated that He whom they sought would be born in Jerusalem.

Recall the words in St. Matthew's Gospel: ". . . behold, there came wise men from the east to Jerusalem, Saying, Where is he that is born King of the Jews? for we have seen his star . . . and are come to worship him" (Matt. 2:1-2). They asked this question of wise men at the court of Herod, the Jewish king. Remember, too, that Herod was not a real king in the ancient line of David. He was a puppet placed on the throne of Jerusalem by the power of the Roman Emperor, Caesar Augustus. We can guess how Herod reacted when he heard the news of the Three Wise Men's search! He was frightened!

St. Matthew tells us what happened: "When Herod . . . had heard these things, he was troubled, and all Jerusalem with him. And when he had gathered all the chief priests and scribes . . . together, he demanded of them where Christ should be born" (Matt. 2:3-4). (Remember that "Christ" was the Jewish term for the great descendant of David whom the prophets had foretold would one day be born to be the Saviour of His people.) "And they said unto him, In Bethlehem of Judea: for thus it is written by the prophet. And thou Bethlehem, in the land of Juda: for out of thee shall come a Governor, that shall rule my people Israel" (Matt. 2:5-6).

The prophet referred to was Micah of the Old Testament. If we read the second verse of the fifth chapter of Micah, we find these interesting words: "But thou, Bethlehem . . . though thou be little among the thousands of Judah, yet out of thee shall . . . come forth . . . that is to be ruler in Israel."

Hearing of this ancient prophecy of Micah, the Wise Men left Jerusalem in haste to go to Bethlehem, four miles away. They found that the only child born there at the time when the star appeared was Jesus, the Son of Mary. They paid their homage to Him and, disobeying Herod's command to return to Jerusalem and notify him who the child was, departed in haste to their own countries by another way.

The crafty, but frightened political hack, Herod, had decided to kill Christ. When the Wise Men did not return, he took no chances of a threat to his own shaky power, and ordered the slaughter of every male child in Bethlehem under the age of two. Joseph and Mary escaped with Jesus by fleeing across the border into Egypt. The evidence, therefore, is beyond question that the story of the visit of the Magi to Christ is absolutely true.

The third question is the most important of all. What does the story of Epiphany mean for us today? It means that God has made Himself known to us best, not in the wonder of the starry heavens, or in any other part of nature, but in a Person like ourselves. Nobody will ever understand what God is like until he lowers his eyes from the heavens and looks into the face of Jesus Christ.

Notice how learning has progressed. It started with astrologers who looked to the stars to explain the mystery of human life. After the ancient astrologers, came the philosophers of Greece and Rome. They looked at *men* and tried to find a set of universal, philosophical laws which would explain human behavior. They and the Old

Testament prophets taught mankind nearly all it knows about the moral law.

Nevertheless God, merely as the embodiment of morality, was too remote for the average man to understand, or to be of help in time of need. We all need a personal Saviour. We need God whom we can visualize and really know. We need God who personally experienced in the flesh the joy and pain of human life. God understood this clearly. That is why He came down into human life in the Person of Jesus Christ our Lord.

So, what Epiphany says to us is this: "No matter how wise you are, no matter how learned or wealthy you may be, you do not know God until you have recognized Him in the face of Jesus Christ." Science can tell us some things about God. Philosophy can tell us other things. But only through faith in Christ, who was all knowledge made flesh, can we behold the only-begotten of the Father, full of grace and truth.

8. Three Qualities of Christ

Think about that strange miracle performed by Christ—the spectacular account of the raising of a man from the dead. It is recounted only in St. Luke's Gospel, chapter seven, verses 11 through 15:

> And it came to pass the day after, that [Jesus] went into a city called Nain . . . Now when he came nigh to the gate of the city, behold, there was a dead man carried out, the only son of his mother, and she was a widow . . . And when the Lord saw her, he had compassion on her, and said unto her, Weep not. And he came and touched the bier: and they that bare him stood still. And he said, Young man, I say unto thee, Arise. And he that was dead sat up, and began to speak. And he delivered him to his mother.

There are three notable things about Jesus in this dramatic story. *Notice how compassionate He was!* He had just ended a long journey. It is probable that Christ was weary with travel. Like any human being, He longed to find a place to rest and be refreshed. Moreover, He was a stranger. This funeral procession had nothing to do with Him. No one would have blamed Him in the least had He quietly passed it by in order to take care of His own needs.

Unlike many situations described in the Gospels, not a soul asked Him for any help. Yet when He realized the tragedy before Him, He did not wait to be asked. This was no ordinary funeral. Here was a poor woman, already a widow, who now had lost her only son! No wonder Jesus "had compassion on her." This was close to the ultimate in pathos.

What is so wonderful in this incident is the assurance it brings that God cares greatly for us. The divine response is instantaneous. It does not wait upon conditions to be fulfilled. As Jesus was, so God is. If our Lord had compassion on a nameless stranger, how easy it is to believe that God is concerned about each one of us. Have no fear. God knows all our needs. He feels our secret anxiety. He is aware of our slightest worry. He never forgets us. Whenever trouble comes, our heavenly Father is deeply moved with pity, just as was His Son. The compassion we see here is the same compassion that God has for each of us.

Notice next that Jesus *acted with authority*. It is almost overwhelming in its simplicity. He did not call out. He did not ask a lot of useless questions. Instead He came quietly and touched the bier: and they that bore the dead man stood still. Not a word had been spoken. Yet, He, a total stranger, commanded such instant respect that when He interrupted at such a solemn moment no one was angry or amazed.

Christ had a powerful influence upon people which set Him apart. He called fishermen. They left their nets forever. Crowds followed Him. Even the proud Roman, Pontius Pilate, marvelled at His dignity. The Jewish people said of Him, He speaks not as a scribe or a Pharisee, but as one having authority.

Nor was the acceptance without hesitation of His intrusion into

48

the private grief of a strange woman the end of Jesus' commanding action. We would have doubtless offered sympathy. Our Lord did nothing of the kind. Instead He spoke with authority, "And he said, Young man, I say unto thee, Arise. And he that was dead sat up, and began to speak."

When people ask us why we believe that Jesus was divine, we can give many reasons for our faith. The chief reason is the Resurrection. But the Gospel is filled with many demonstrations which show Him to be unique. Among these is the undeniable effect He had on those who saw Him in the flesh. He left no doubt in anybody's mind that He possessed authority beyond that of ordinary human beings.

Finally, Christ had a *life-giving quality* about Him! In this story He literally restored a dead man's life. Yet think what new life He brought to this desolate widow! One of the most touching phrases in the New Testament is "And he delivered him to his mother." A moment earlier her whole life had been shrouded in despair. Now she knew joy and thanksgiving.

Our Lord said, "I am come that [men] might have life, and that they might have it more abundantly" (John 10:10). Go through your Gospels. What do you find? Lepers are healed. The paralyzed take up their beds and walk. The demented are cured. A Roman centurion's servant is made well. The daughter of Jairus is brought out of shock. A woman with a crooked spine is given the power to stand straight. A blind man received his sight. A soldier's ear that was cut off by one of Jesus' disciples was restored. These were all examples of His remarkable power to relieve physical suffering.

Yet that was not the only kind of new life that our Lord gave while He was on earth. He gave hope to the discouraged. He gave the desire and power to be righteous to those who were sinful. He gave love to the unwanted. He gave a vision of a new heaven and a new earth to His disciples. All these things and more He did in the three years of His ministry. Does any man read about Christ and not say this man performed wonders?

What is told us in the Gospels about the power of Jesus to give life is nothing compared to what He has done since those days for millions of people who have believed in Him. He enabled an African named Augustine to break away from a life of lust and become a saint, whose vision of the City of God still stirs the souls of men. He took a highborn wastrel named Francis of Assisi and turned him into a living illustration of Christian charity. He took a monk named Luther and gave him the strength to reform the corruption of the Church itself. He took an organ-playing Greek scholar named Albert Schweitzer and turned him into the greatest medical missionary of our modern day.

These are a few of the great names to whom Christ gave life. More important than any of these, He took countless men and women whose names we shall never know, and He lifted their heads bowed down with many sorrows, and by the faith that He inspired He gave them strength to overcome the weight of all their burdens. This same thing He can do for us.

Compassion, authority, and the power to give life, these are qualities of Jesus. We can feel all three as we grow in knowledge and love of Him.

9. The Compassion of Christ

In the observance of Lent we join a multitude which figuratively journeys with Christ, and stands at last before the Cross on which He died.

St. Luke's Gospel shows us a very dramatic scene which interrupted our Lord's journey. Jesus and His disciples were going up to Jerusalem. It was a fateful journey. Our Lord knew that it would end in His death. As they approached Jericho, a great crowd recognized Him. Much noise went up from the multitude. A blind beggar asked what was happening. He was told "that Jesus of Nazareth passeth by." Then he cried out, "Jesus, thou son of David, have mercy on me." Several of the disciples, trying to clear passage for the Master, told the beggar to be quiet. He shouted even louder. And Jesus stood and commanded him to be brought unto Him. When he was come near, Jesus asked, "What wilt thou that I shall do unto thee? And he said, Lord, that I may receive my sight. And Jesus said . . . Receive thy sight: thy faith hath saved thee" (Luke 18:41-2).

Notice first that a great commotion took place when Jesus of Nazareth passed by! Whenever He appeared things began to happen! On the night of His birth, angels sang; shepherds hurried; and Wise Men rode. Wherever He talked crowds gathered. On Palm Sunday travelers tore branches from trees and strawed them in His way. On Easter Day people began running to tell the news of the Resurrection. After Whitsunday, the Church overthrew the Roman world.

Christ always causes men to get excited. This is the reason why the Church makes so much of Lent. The purpose of Lent is to stir up a commotion by focusing attention sharply on Jesus. The call of Lent is to lessen worldly concerns and join the throng going to see the Lord pass by. Nobody can get close to Christ and not become a better person.

Think for a moment about the blind beggar. Each one of us is much like him. We huddle by the roadside of life, blinded to the beauty of what we can really be. Yet that blind beggar must be admired. He was a courageous and determined man. He knew that he needed help. When he found out that Jesus was passing through his city, what did he do? He began to shout, "Thou son of David, have mercy on me." Even when he was elbowed out of the way, he did not give up trying. An obstacle made him only cry out more loudly than before.

There is a lesson in this for every one of us. We should never permit obstacles to blot out our hope that God will help us. How easy it is to give in to discouragements! We sometimes feel so sorry for ourselves that we will no longer try. Everyone has unused capacities of which he does not dream. We have to make the first great effort to get close to God. If we dare to try, and when we fail, dare to try again, we go far in finding the help we need.

Notice something else in this story: "They which went before rebuked [the beggar], that he should hold his peace." This means that the disciples themselves tried to stand between this needy man and God! The disciples undoubtedly meant well. Jesus was on a journey and He had many problems on His mind. Had He not just said, "Behold, we go up to Jerusalem, and all things that are written by the prophets concerning the Son of man shall be accomplished"? His followers were trying to make things easier for Christ.

It is also possible that they were protecting themselves. To stop for a blind beggar meant inconvenience and delay. Yet no matter how they rationalized their motives, the fact remained that they pushed a needy human being aside. They tried to set up a wall between one man and another man. In fact, they were sealing off a man from God!

When the Church has been most truly the Church, it has always pulled down walls. It has lived up to the vision of the prophet Isaiah and St. John the Baptist:

> . . . Prepare ye the way of the Lord, make straight in the desert a highway for our God. Every valley shall be exalted, and every mountain and hill shall be made low: and the crooked shall be made straight, and the rough places plain: And the glory of the Lord shall be revealed, and all flesh shall see it together . . . .
>
> (Isaiah 40:3-5)

So let us take this lesson to heart and reach out our hands in love to all sorts and conditions of men.

Now we come to the most beautiful part of this Gospel:

> And Jesus stood, and commanded [the beggar] to be brought unto him: and when he was come near, he asked him, Saying, What wilt thou that I shall do unto thee? And he said, Lord, that I may receive my sight. And Jesus said unto him, Receive thy sight: thy faith hath saved thee.
>
> (Luke 18:40-2)

It is truly marvelous that anyone, even Jesus Christ, could be so considerate of others when He knew that in a few short days He Himself would die. Christ did not allow His own troubles to blot out His concern for other people. The test of true human greatness comes when our personal burdens are the most difficult. If anyone at that moment can still see another person's need and offer a helping hand, that man is truly great.

Yet Jesus was never a sentimentalist. Notice what He said to the blind beggar: "What wilt thou that I shall do unto thee?" He wanted to hear from the man's own lips what it was that he wanted most. He could only do for the beggar what the beggar wanted and believed with all his heart that Christ could do for him. If the blind man had only had faith enough to ask for a few pennies, that is all that Jesus could have done for him. What we receive is limited not by God's capacity to give, but by our capacity to receive. To know what we really need and to have faith in God's ability to give it are the secrets to the answers to our prayers.

This portion of the Gospel is about the importance of being big. Christ was big enough to journey up to Jerusalem to face a cross. A blind beggar was big enough not to give up when he was shoved aside. Jesus was big enough to be merciful to the needy when He had troubles of His own. And that needy man's faith was big enough to believe that God could help him.

Each one of us must dare to take a giant step, big enough to be worthy of our God.

10. The Meaning of Christ's Temptations

John the Baptist hailed Jesus, at His baptism, as the Messiah, and almost immediately after this great event, He was subjected to forty days of grave temptation.

The devil tempted Jesus in three different ways, and each one of us is tempted constantly in the same fashion. Let us look at each temptation. The ordeal of Christ will help us to understand ourselves.

The first words of the devil were very clever: "If thou be the Son of God, command that these stones be made bread" (Matt. 4:3). Satan is the original "hidden persuader." Notice his diabolic use of psychology. The devil slyly attempts to create doubt: he says, "*If* thou be the Son of God." The devil never concedes truth. Temptation always is strong when we are uncertain. It was a poor tactic for Satan to use on Christ. Jesus knew that He was the Son of God. The only thing He was not yet clear about was exactly how to begin His ministry of salvation.

Notice also that the devil struck first at what he thought was a weak spot in Jesus. Our Lord had been fasting. He was hungry. So the suggestion is made, "Satisfy your hunger by turning a few stones into bread." This too was very tricky. Not only was Jesus tempted to provide food for Himself, but He was tempted to win the souls of men by giving food to hungry people. How easy it would have been for Christ to gain a following, if He provided bread! Every politician since Nero has understood how to win public acclaim by offering a free living to the crowd. We remember that Hitler did it. Khrushchev is doing it today. In any election year in this country, one can hear some of our presidential candidates do it again. The price tag is always carefully concealed. No giveaway program is ever free. The price is always twofold: surrender of personal freedom, and higher taxes.

Jesus rejected this temptation without a moment's hesitation. He knew more about the real needs of men than the devil did. Recall how He replied, "Man shall not live by bread alone" (Matt. 4:4). These words are certainly among the most profound ever uttered by human tongue. What do men live by? They live by love. They live by satisfying, daily work. They live by dedication to great causes. They live by faith in God. If all we search for in life is material security, we will wind up being wretched. This will be true, even if we get it. Do not misunderstand. One of the important needs of man is a good material standard of living. But it is only one need. And in spite of present-day emphasis on it, it is less important than many spiritual needs.

54

Christ's reply to the devil should remind the Christian Church what its real task is. The Church is not a settlement house; its clergy are not primarily social workers; its program does not center in providing better housing or more secure jobs. The central concern of the Church is to proclaim God and to create Faith in His eternal goodness.

There is a constant temptation today, when men are struggling all over the world to better their conditions, for the Church to identify the Gospel with mankind's material aspirations. Obviously, the Gospel has deep social, political and economic implications. But when the last word has been said, the unique responsibility of the Christian religion is to help John Jones and Mary Smith, as individual souls, to trust God and be worthy of eternal salvation.

Look now at the second temptation. Once again the devil makes a suggestion which begins with "if." "Then the devil taketh him up into the holy city, and setteth him on a pinnacle of the temple. And saith unto him, *If* thou be the Son of God, cast thyself down . . ." (Matt. 4:5-6). This time he tries to seduce Jesus' will power by quoting Psalm 91. "For it is written, He shall give his angels charge concerning thee: and in their hands they shall bear thee up, lest at any time thou dash thy foot against a stone" (Matt. 4:6/Psalm 91:11-12). This passage gave rise to Shakespeare's famous saying in *The Merchant of Venice:* "The devil can cite Scripture for his purpose."

One of the minor crosses which most churchmen, especially the clergy, have to bear is the way people with an axe to grind quote Scripture to prove their point. Usually they quote, as did the devil in this case, a passage out of its context. Just remember that "a text out of its context is a pretext!"

The devil picked the wrong person to beat over the head with a passage from the Bible. Jesus knew the Old Testament by heart, so His reply to the devil's second temptation was a quotation from Deuteronomy: "Ye shall not tempt the Lord your God" (Deut. 6:16).

What was this second temptation? It was the enticement to win a quick following by doing a spectacular stunt. Hitler set fire to the Parliament Building in Berlin, blamed it on the Communists, and frightened the German people into giving him dictatorial power. Just before Khrushchev visited this country a few years ago, he launched a missile around the moon. There is no denying that such spectacular acts have enormous propaganda value. In today's world we can expect both Russia and the United States to use propaganda to impress people with every notable achievement.

There is one great flaw in spectacular publicity. It always beclouds the principal issue of the moment by distracting attention from the main event to a side show.

If Christ had jumped from the top of the temple in Jerusalem, He certainly would have made a name for Himself immediately throughout the length and breadth of Israel. But He knew that once you start jumping from steeples, you dare not stop. The followers you win expect you to repeat the performance. If you do not, they quickly lose interest. Whoever takes a ride on the merry-go-round of artificial publicity may win a brass ring or two, but nothing is more monotonous than riding a merry-go-round for the rest of your life.

So Christ rejected the temptation to win a following by achieving quick notoriety. Instead, He chose to build His Church by carefully selecting twelve inconspicuous Jews. These men He patiently taught. He slowly stamped upon them His ideals, His faith, and His obedience to God.

To many people the Church always seems to be behind the times. The remarkable fact, however, is that it is still around. Precious little else has survived two thousand years of human history. Jesus understood that no one can nudge God to move a little faster. He has no need to hurry. If the devil had known his Scriptures as well as Christ did, he would have remembered that the 90th Psalm begins, "Lord, thou hast been our dwelling place in all generations ... For a thousand years in thy sight are but as yesterday when it is past, and as a watch in the night" (Psalm 90:1/4).

The Kingdom of God cannot be built on headlines in the news.

The third temptation that came to Christ was to grasp after power to achieve His goal. "Again, the devil taketh him up into an exceeding high mountain, and sheweth him all the kingdoms of the

56

world, and the glory of them; And saith unto him, All these things will I give thee, if thou wilt fall down and worship me" (Matt. 4:8-9).

It is interesting to observe that by now the devil realized that he could not tempt Jesus by sowing the seeds of doubt. This time Satan did not start out by saying, "*If* thou be the Son of God." He dropped that approach as a waste of time. Christ knew that He was the Son of God, and by now the devil knew that He knew it. Instead, Satan made a bold frontal attack on what he considered to be Christ's likeliest weakness. He knew that Jesus wanted to make salvation available to men everywhere in the world. Yet He was by birth a Jew. Up until the time of Christ, no Jew could conceive of God as being impartially interested in all sorts and conditions of men. The devil realized that Jesus at this early point in His ministry had not yet decided how to reach the Gentile world with His Gospel. So he offered Christ power over all mankind.

See the desperate craftiness of Satan. He had gained a great measure of power over man when Adam and Eve fell from grace. He also clearly recognized that Jesus, the Son of God, was the first human being likely to break the power of man's Original Sin. Christ was the most serious challenge the devil had ever encountered in his struggle for men's souls. Indeed, he was the ultimate test of Satan's power. He had to break Jesus, or be broken by Him. That is why Satan was desperate. As a last-ditch effort, he offered Christ a baited trap. His proposal was the slickest ever made in the history of mankind. Satan offered to give Christ power over all the kingdoms of the earth on one condition. All Jesus would need to do was to fall down and worship the devil. Once this was done, Satan would have destroyed Christ as the Son of man. From that moment he would have controlled mankind through Christ.

You have to give the devil credit! Had he succeeded, not only would there have been no salvation for man's soul, but a blow would have been struck at the integrity of God's own Person. It is no exaggeration to say that this third temptation was one of the decisive moments in the history of creation. If Jesus had accepted the devil's offer, God would have been destroyed.

This dreadful effrontery quickly brought the temptation of Christ to an end. Jesus not only rejected the devil's offer, but dismissed him from His presence. Listen to Christ's words: "Get thee hence, Satan: for it is written, Thou shalt worship the Lord thy God, and him only shalt thou serve" (Matt. 4:10).

The worst temptation that can come to any man is the ambition to possess power over the lives of other people. Life provides, in small or great degree, that all men have responsibilities toward some other people. Husbands and wives have a responsibility to each other and to their children. How easy it is to transform responsibility into the exercise of power over the members of our families. All of us have seen children destroyed by the misused power of their parents. An employer has a responsibility to his employees. Likewise, workers have a responsibility to management and to the public. Neither one should abuse power. In years gone by, an employer had such frightful power that he could grind his workers in poverty. Now the worm has turned. Organized labor has enormous power. One of the great problems today is how this power will be used!

Government has power. Some governments, like those of Russia and China, have absolute power. Ours is a government of checks and balances—total power is given to no one part. So far this has proved to be the best guarantee of individual freedom. Because the problems our nation faces today are very baffling, there is a tendency to look increasingly to Washington to solve them. Some of this is inevitable. However, Americans should remember that every time the Federal Government assumes a responsibility, more power is concentrated there. Such a tendency slowly erodes freedom.

Power always contains the seeds of its own destruction. Lord Acton said, in 1887, in a letter to Bishop Creighton, "Power tends to corrupt; absolute power corrupts absolutely." Power destroyed ancient Rome. Power destroyed the mediaeval Church. Power destroyed Czarist Russia. Power, I believe, will eventually destroy the Communist governments.

Christ understood the spiritual danger of power. He would have none of it. Instead, He began the work of salvation with a reliance

58

on God's love. Love is the central commandment of Christian Faith. Love serves. It does not coerce. Love arouses a response of love. Power creates antagonism. That is why the cornerstone of Christ's kingdom is anchored supremely in love.

The one great problem of human existence is to learn how to love.

11. Gethsemane and the Cross

In many respects the scene of Christ suffering in the garden on the night before His Crucifixion is even more agonizing than His suffering and death upon the Cross. This is so because on Good Friday Christ betrayed no fear or doubt. In Gethsemane, on the other hand, His terror is so great that He sweat blood in anticipation of His coming terrible ordeal.

Let us go back for a moment to Palm Sunday in order to see clearly what events brought Christ to the fearsome garden where He was betrayed by Judas.

How was it possible for great crowds to welcome Jesus triumphantly into Jerusalem on that great Sunday, and within six days cry for His death upon the Cross? The answer is a simple one. The Jewish people yearned for a great national leader to emerge who would overthrow the government of Rome. Ever since the days of the great King David, who lived a thousand years before Jesus, the Jews lived in the promise that someday another David would set their country free. All of the great Hebrew prophets had proclaimed that someday the Messiah would come.

When the Palm Sunday crowds hailed Jesus as their King, it was this long hoped-for Messiah that they believed they saw in Him. If Jesus had allowed Himself that first Palm Sunday to be anointed as the King of the Jews, the majority of Israelites would have risen in rebellion against the hated Roman Empire. If He had acted like the King they expected their Messiah to be, there probably would have been savage slaughter on both sides, but there would have been no Cross, no Easter Day, and no new religion born which could speak to men of every nation on the earth.

The kind of Messiah the Jews expected was not the kind of Messiah Jesus wanted to be. What did the Jews expect of their Messiah?

First, that he look like a king. Obviously, Jesus fulfilled this important qualification. We should never picture Christ as a physical weakling. He stood head and shoulders over His fellow Jews. Hard labor as a carpenter had turned his muscles into steel. He was broad-shouldered and large-chested. Moreover, there was something about His face and stature that always caught the imagination of a crowd. Wherever He walked, crowds gathered and followed Him. The fact is that Jesus looked like a Jewish King.

Second, the Messiah was supposed to make every Jew rich. He would possess a magical quality about Him, so that when He touched stones in a field, they would turn into loaves of bread. He had to be a wonder-worker, a miracle man, with power to give a downtrodden people the luxuries they dearly desired. The whole country knew of the miracle of the loaves and fishes. Naturally it was expected that Jesus could not only feed people, but also make them well-to-do.

Third, He had to be a healer. The sick would be made well by the miraculous power of the Messiah's healing gifts. Jesus was well-known for His healing acts. The sick and the crippled gathered in great numbers wherever it was known that He would be. Consequently, He fulfilled this qualification of a Messiah in the people's mind.

Finally, the Messiah had to raise an army and drive out the hated Roman soldiers.

All these things the Palm Sunday crowds expected Jesus to do. Instead, He drove the Jewish money-changers out of the temple. Immediately afterward, He refused the Crown of Israel at the hand of Judas Iscariot, and disappeared into the crowds.

Now the twelve disciples also expected Jesus to do all four of these things. Imagine how chagrined they were when He turned His wrath, not against Rome, but against the sacred customs of the temple! To one disciple at least, it seemed that Jesus was after all only one more untrustworthy, wandering prophet. That disciple, of course, was Judas. At the end of the first Palm Sunday, Judas had decided to betray his Master into the power of His enemies.

So, right at the beginning of Holy Week, we see the Cross. Jesus knew what He was doing. Already He knew that He could not be the kind of Messiah the Jewish people longed to have. On Palm Sunday He accepted the first full responsibility of the Cross by sacrificing the thousand-year-old Jewish idea of what the Messiah would be like. Knowing the disappointment of the crowds who had hailed Him as their King, knowing also the bitter confusion that now existed among His very disciples, He needed a quiet place to think over His next important move. So He slipped out of Jerusalem and went to the home of a friend, Simon the leper, in Bethany. Here He remained until the feast of the Passover was to be celebrated.

Here in this house a further incident took place which disturbed the disciples and infuriated Judas, who was the treasurer of the twelve. He was the practical businessman of affairs. So, when a woman came bearing an alabaster box of precious ointment and poured it all out in a loving, generous gesture of her admiration for Christ, it is recorded that the disciples had indignation, saying, "To what purpose is this waste?" (Matt. 26:8). Then Jesus shocked His disciples by claiming that although the woman did not realize it, she was really anointing His body for His burial. That was all that Judas could take. He left Simon the leper's house in anger and went to the chief priests to arrange the betrayal of our Lord.

Here, in this incident, we see the Cross looming large again. Jesus knows by now that to do His Father's will, His life must somehow be sacrificed. But on this Tuesday night in the first Holy Week, He was calm, relaxed, and gracious to His dearest friends. We need to ask ourselves how we might act when the grave dangers of life come close to us.

On Thursday several of Jesus' disciples asked where He desired to eat the Passover:

> And he said, Go into the city to such a man, and say unto him, The Master saith, My time is at hand; I will keep the passover at thy house with my disciples.
>
> And the disciples did as Jesus had appointed them; and they made ready the passover. Now when the even was come, he sat down with the twelve.
>
> And as they were eating, Jesus took bread, and blessed it, and brake it, and gave it to the disciples, and said, Take, eat; this is my body. And he took the cup, and gave thanks, and gave it to them, saying, Drink ye all of it; For this is my blood of the new testament, which is shed for many for the remission of sins.
>
> But I say unto you, I will not drink henceforth of this fruit of the vine, until that day when I drink it new with you in my Father's kingdom. And when they had sung an hymn, they went out into the mount of Olives.
>
> (Matt. 26:18-20, 26-30)

Notice how the Cross becomes the central theme as Jesus breaks bread and blesses wine during the Last Supper, the first Eucharist. The bread becomes His body broken, the wine His blood shed for the salvation of mankind. Thus on Maundy Thursday night, and forever after where Christians are celebrating Holy Communion, the Cross is central to Christian Faith. We know that it is a cross over which Christ has triumphed. To us the Eucharist is an act of highest joy. But to Christ's disciples the Last Supper must have seemed so filled with the dreadful promise of suffering for Christ that they were chilled to their marrow as they heard His words, "This is my body . . . this is my blood!"

The disciples had followed Jesus for many different reasons. All were struck by His magnificent appearance. All were impressed by His miracles and acts of healing. All were deeply moved by His eloquent preaching. But we must remember that every single one expected Him to be only a son of David—a great, earthly King of Israel. What did they hope for? A better life for Jewish people. A decent government. And two of them at least expected to be elevated to high positions of worldly authority or rank when He came into His kingdom upon earth. These two were James and John, who sent their mother to inquire of Christ if they could sit on His right hand and His left hand when He became King.

Had it not been for the Resurrection, each one of these men, with the possible exception of the beloved disciple St. John, probably would have gone back to his former work after the death of Christ.

So there was a cross in the events which led up to Gethsemane for each of them too. They were already being called upon to sacrifice everything in their lives that they held dear, to take up their own crosses and follow Him.

We need to realize that this demand is made of every Christian since Gethsemane. When we accept Christ as our Lord and Saviour, we accept the principle of the Cross in our whole life. The road to our salvation is the road of sacrifice of all we hold dear for the sake of Jesus Christ and His Church. We no longer live for ourselves. We live only that God's plan of salvation will go forward in our generation. He who shirks the Cross does not truly follow Him "who died upon the Cross."

We come now to Gethsemane itself. Leaving the house where the Last Supper was eaten, Jesus goes with some of His disciples unto this famous garden.

> And he took with him Peter and the two sons of Zebedee, and began to be sorrowful and very heavy. Then saith he unto them, My soul is exceeding sorrowful, even unto death: tarry ye here, and watch with me.
>
> And he went a little farther, and fell on his face, and prayed, saying, O my Father, if it be possible, let this cup pass from me: nevertheless not as I will, but as thou wilt.
>
> And he cometh unto the disciples, and findeth them asleep, and saith unto Peter, What, could ye not watch with me one hour? Watch and pray, that ye enter not into temptation: the spirit indeed is willing, but the flesh is weak.

He went away again the second time, and prayed, saying, O my Father, if this cup may not pass away from me, except I drink it, thy will be done.

And he came and found them asleep again: for their eyes were heavy. And he left them, and went away again, and prayed the third time, saying the same words.

Then cometh he to his disciples, and saith unto them, Sleep on now, and take your rest: behold, the hour is at hand, and the Son of man is betrayed into the hands of sinners.

(Matt. 26:37-45)

Here we witness a scene which I think is more terrible than the Crucifixion itself. It is frightening because we witness the soul of Christ shrinking in fright from what lay ahead of Him. On Good Friday He was the most composed of men. But in Gethsemane's Garden, Christ sweat blood as He struggled to find some alternative to His own death. I am sure that He wanted nothing more than to get up on His legs and run away from the city of Jerusalem.

It is a bitter commentary on our Lord's Passion, too, that He received no comfort from His disciples. While He prayed, they fell asleep. Here is a further aspect of the Cross. When we are in trouble, what a comfort it is to know that our loved ones are near and ready to help us share our suffering. It is hard enough to go through difficult times. But it is infinitely harder when we have to face suffering all alone.

Christ looked with agony upon His sleeping companions. As we look back, the most awful words ever to come from the lips of Jesus were these: "Could ye not watch with me one hour?"

I think we should all remember this scene. God in Christ needed us. He still needs us today. God longs to know that we love Him. If we do not show our love, then He has failed in all He tried to do by suffering and dying for us. "Could ye not watch one hour?" These are words which should haunt us when we fail to go to church or to say our daily prayers!

Finally, His terrible hour in the Garden of Gethsemane was ended. Fear left the heart of Jesus. He knew what He had to do.

64

His mind was at last made up. Now His phenomenal calm had returned to Him!

And just as He wakened His disciples, Judas entered the garden followed by a group of temple soldiers. But these are soldiers of the high priest, not Romans. They have been sent by Caiaphas to bring Jesus for questioning before the Jewish Sanhedrin. The Roman government was not yet involved. The quarrel was still a Jewish religious and political affair.

Notice the dreadful irony of the way Christ was betrayed. Judas stepped forward and betrayed his Master with a kiss! The slyness and the cunning of Judas send chills down one's spine. He did not have the courage to trust Christ in these fateful hours. Neither did he have the courage to accuse Him openly. Instead, he hid himself and his dreadful act by camouflaging his betrayal under the sign of deepest friendship. He betrayed Christ, not with the pointing finger of accusation. He betrayed Him with a kiss!

Need I say that you and I are tempted daily to do the same? Not one of us would ever think of saying, "I do not believe in Jesus Christ." Yet too often, as we say with our lips, "I believe," we betray Christ in our hearts. We betray Him whenever we adjust our loyalties so that we can live comfortably both in the sinful world and in the kingdom of God. On Sundays or occasionally at other times, we are Christians. But frequently, in our homes and at our jobs, we act as if we were no different from the pagans who surround us. This is betraying Jesus with a kiss! This is Gethsemane's final Cross brought up-to-date and made fashionable today. He who would not be another Judas, let him examine how real his loyalty to Christ is at all times and in all places.

As Jesus is taken into custody, we watch Him walk toward the Cross with head held high and spirit strong. He won the battle of Holy Week, which was to be true to the mission His heavenly Father had sent Him into the world to do. He had been sorely tempted from Palm Sunday until Maundy Thursday. At last the temptations of Jesus were at an end. The triumph over the Cross had already been won in His inner spirit. The joy of Easter Day was already in Christ's heart.

12. Christ's Trial and the Cross

When Jesus was betrayed by Judas Iscariot, He was immediately taken into custody by temple guards. Within an hour He was being tried by Caiaphas, the high priest, and by members of the Jewish Sanhedrin. This trial lasted about three hours. It took place in the Council Chamber of the Sanhedrin.

Two things should be remembered about this Temple Trial. Caiaphas and the Jewish Council could hear only religious cases. They had no jurisdiction in political or civil affairs. They could only judge whether or not a man had broken a religious law of the Jews.

Second, Caiaphas, the high priest, and most of the Sanhedrin wanted to kill Jesus. They had long looked upon Him as a dangerous revolutionary. Finally, just the Sunday before He had wrecked the tables of the money-changers in the sacred temple. However, Jewish religious courts no longer could pronounce the death penalty. That right belonged exclusively to the Roman governor.

So the high priest had a serious problem on his hands. He had to devise a way to accuse Jesus of something serious enough to condemn Him before a Jewish court, and at the same time twist the accusation so that it would sound like a crime which threatened the Roman rule of Israel.

At first Caiaphas had little success. A number of witnesses were paraded before the Sanhedrin, but none of them could think of anything serious that Jesus had done.

Finally, about two o'clock in the morning, two witnesses testified as follows: "This fellow said, I am able to destroy the temple of God, and to build it in three days" (Matt. 26:61). Yet even this alleged threat to destroy religious property was only hearsay evidence and came to nothing.

66

It was then that Caiaphas realized that he had to play his trump card. He wanted to ensnare Jesus into an admission which could be called "blasphemy" by the Jews, and "treason" to the Roman Empire. Consequently, he forced Jesus to answer a loaded question. Caiaphas addressed these words to Jesus: "I adjure thee by the living God . . . tell us whether thou be the Christ, the Son of God" (Matt. 26:63). There was dead silence in the Council Chamber. This was a grave moment. If Jesus answered "Yes," He would be guilty of blasphemy. If He answered "No," He would have spoken a lie.

Finally Jesus spoke, "Thou hast said." This was bad enough—but listen to what He went on to say: "Nevertheless I say . . . Hereafter shall ye see the Son of man sitting on the right hand of power, and coming in the clouds of heaven" (Matt. 26:64). He had not only accepted the title of Messiah. He had threatened the authority of the high priest.

Now notice how this first trial ended. "Then the high priest rent his clothes, saying, He hath spoken blasphemy; what further need have we of witnesses? behold, now ye have heard his blasphemy. What think ye? They answered and said, He is guilty of death" (Matt. 26:65-6). So Caiaphas had accomplished his first purpose. Jesus stood condemned to death for blasphemy in the eyes of Jewish law. The only trouble was that the Jews no longer could kill a man for blasphemy. So Caiaphas had to find some way to accuse Jesus before a Roman court on a charge serious enough to condemn Him to death. The high priest and his friends spent the rest of the night preparing the strategy of Christ's later trial before Pontius Pilate. They decided to twist Christ's testimony that He was the Messiah into a claim that He was the political King of the Jews. As such, He might start a revolt against Rome, and thus would be a constant threat to Roman rule.

Meanwhile one of the saddest moments in the trial occurred. As Jesus was being led away, His eyes suddenly fell on Peter, sitting huddled before the fire. Peter was the only one of the twelve who dared to follow Jesus to the trial. Several people recognized him as a follower of Jesus. Three times Peter denied that he ever knew

Christ. The third time, the cock crew, and Peter suddenly remembered what Jesus had said to him at the Last Supper when he had boasted that though others deserted Jesus, he would be faithful even unto death. Christ had replied, "Before the cock crow twice, thou shalt deny me thrice" (Mark 14:30). Now in shame Peter looked up, as Jesus was being led away, into the sorrowing eyes of Christ. Neither spoke. Then sobbing, Peter fled into the night. He went into hiding and did not reappear until Easter morning.

As the trial of Jesus progressed, Judas Iscariot realized that he had gone too far. He never intended that Jesus be killed. At the most he thought He might be beaten with a rod and let go. It had never occurred to him that Caiaphas would take Jesus before a Roman judge on a charge which carried with it the death penalty. When he saw what had happened, Judas took the thirty pieces of silver to the temple priests and asked them to take it back and free Christ. They merely laughed at him, and said, "What is that to us?" In fear and humiliation, Judas threw down the silver and went out into the night and hanged himself.

Early on Friday morning Jesus was brought before the Roman governor, Pontius Pilate, for His second trial. The charge was that He called Himself "The King of the Jews." It was devilishly simple. To the Jews, it was the height of "blasphemy." To the Romans, it was "treason."

This Roman trial will always be a remarkable testimony to Christ. At every moment in it, He is a towering figure of dignity and calm.

It is obvious from the start that Pilate is enormously impressed by Jesus. He had no desire to kill Him, and least of all did he wish to please Caiaphas, the high priest, whom he had ample reason not to trust. It is fair to say that Pontius Pilate did everything he could to save Jesus from the Cross.

First, he offered to have Him beaten and let go. This did not satisfy the Jews, and they set up a clamor for a sterner penalty. Then he offered to let a prisoner go because of the Passover. Instead of Jesus, the crowd chose Barabbas, a convicted murderer. Third, Pilate tried to shift the trial back to a religious judge. He inter-

68

rupted the hearing to send Jesus to Herod, the puppet Jewish king who had been placed on the throne of David by the Roman authority. Herod went through the formality of questioning Christ, but since he had neither authority to judge civil or religious matters, he sent Jesus back to Pontius Pilate.

Meanwhile Pilate's wife had besought her husband to let Jesus go. She had dreamed about Him the previous night, and she was greatly disturbed lest Pilate condemn Him unjustly.

Finally the trial was resumed. Pilate at last put it up to the Jewish crowd: "What will ye that I should do to Jesus, who is called the Christ?" The mob yelled, "Crucify Him, crucify Him!"

It was then that Pontius Pilate called for water. In a dramatic gesture, he washed his hands and said, "I will have nothing to do with the death of this just man; see ye to it." He intended to step out of the picture forever. Instead, he stepped right into the center of the Nicene Creed.

Pilate should be a warning to all of us. He was a decent man, who wanted to be a good governor. He lacked only one quality. He did not have the inward courage to stand up for the right. He knew that Jesus had done nothing worthy of death. He should have thrown the case out of court. Instead, he was afraid to go against the mob. He tried to rationalize his action by washing his hands publicly of responsibility. The man who wanted to have the world forget his part in Jesus' death, has for twenty centuries been called by name in every worship service of the Christian Church, when the Creed has been repeated: "suffered under Pontius Pilate." The Roman governor who signed Jesus' death warrant is the only human being other than our Lord mentioned in the Creed.

As soon as the trial was over, Jesus was led away. This time He was in the custody of Roman soldiers. They took Him first to a prison. There they stripped Him of His clothes. Then they put a scarlet robe upon Him and platted a crown of thorns. Then they mocked Him with loud laughter, bowing down before Him, and crying, "Hail, King of the Jews!"

No time was lost in carrying out the death sentence. Within a few hours Jesus was led out to the hill of Calvary, along the street that has come to be called "the Way of Sorrows." This last dreadful walk taken by our Lord as He was forced to carry His own cross is recalled for us in the devotions of the "Way of the Cross."

The trial of Christ tells us many things about God's dignity and man's weaknesses. I wonder how we would have acted had we been there when the Son of God was put on trial? There is no need to ask! The trial of Christ continues to this day. And you and I are there!

13. The Meaning of the Passion

All human kings, at some time or other in their lives, suffer the agonies of physical or mental torment. Our Lord, too, passed through the dark valley of suffering, especially during that period commemorated in the Church Year as Passiontide, the two weeks preceding Easter. (Many churches veil their crosses in purple to mark this season.)

Think what anguish it brought to Jesus to know that one of His own disciples was plotting against Him! Reflect upon the way He must have been hurt when Peter, His closest friend, denied that he knew Him! Think of His realization of futility when the very crowds, who once had hailed Him as their king, clamored for His crucifixion! Imagine what thoughts must have crossed His mind as He saw the avarice of a friend, the greed of the high priests, the personal ambitions of Pontius Pilate, the fickleness of the man in the street, and the lukewarm loyalty of His followers all conspire to condemn Him to death!

Then upon all this mental anguish was heaped the humiliation He endured before the Roman soldiers, the beatings He received with the bastinado, and finally the awful agony of His last hours upon the Cross.

Worst of all, it happened to One who had done nothing but good.

In the Passion of Jesus, the manifold forms in which evil strikes at men descended all at once upon one Person. The Passion Play will forever remain the most moving spectacle of all time, because everyone recognizes in it the story of human life in its darkest hours. Whoever has beheld it has been forced to admit that

> Towering o'er the wrecks of time;
> All the light of sacred story
> Gathers round its head sublime.
>
> Hymn 336, *The Hymnal* 1940

What is the meaning of the suffering of Jesus Christ? What purpose did it serve?

First of all, no grotesque explanation of the good that was accomplished by the suffering of Jesus can ever satisfy anyone who has a morally sensitive mind. Any theory of the Atonement which makes God out to be a bloodthirsty tyrant who delights in bloodshed, is not the doctrine of the Christian Church.

There have been some bizarre explanations of the suffering of Christ in the past. Here is a theory that held its sway in certain of the denominations for many years:

> The death of Christ was the ransom paid by God to the devil for man's liberation from sin. Satan accepted the offer, thinking to have Christ in his power. But he was outwitted by God, because Christ slipped through his grasp on Easter Day.

This explanation made the devil out a fool; God as a cruel trickster; and Jesus Christ a pitiful scapegoat. Obviously, it is ridiculous!

Here is another, the theory of a man named Anselm:

> Man's sin offended the honor of God. The death of Christ satisfied that honor. Therefore, man had a debt to God paid for him by Christ.

This explanation again outrages a moral man's conception of God. It makes God fickle, easily given to take offense. And it also makes Him cruel.

Such interpretations as these miss the sublimity of what Jesus accomplished by His death. They all seem to suggest that God is an implacable Being who had to see blood to be satisfied, and could not be wholly satisfied until He had the blood of His own Son.

Now turn from that sort of thinking to what a Christian believes is the importance of the suffering of Christ: Christ believed it was right to sacrifice Himself because He knew that only such love could give courage to others who must suffer.

Here is the simple secret of the good that the Passion of Christ accomplished: *The darkest hours of human life can be endured bravely if we are certain that someone who matters to us loves us enough to want to share our sufferings with us.*

If we have an assurance of that kind of love, our suffering is made easier. Whenever anyone puts himself to pain in order to help us, then we are redeemed from cynicism, disillusionment, disbelief, and bitterness. A willing act of loving sacrifice will save us, as nothing else will, from sinking to the lowest levels of our worst natures. Somehow, whenever anybody does make these sacrifices, we actually are moved to become better people ourselves.

During World War II, there was a young Jewish Red Cross orderly by the name of Epstein. He was attached to a small front line fighting unit during the worst of the campaign on Guadalcanal. As most of the unit lay in a foxhole to escape a murderous crossfire of machine gunning from the enemy, one of the Marines who was advancing a little ahead of the others was struck down in the first volley. He lay out in the open, slowly bleeding to death. Young Epstein did not have to crawl out to him, but he did. At the risk of his own life, he stopped the bleeding and got them both back to safety. Those tough Marines wept at the heroism. Twice more Epstein did the same thing for two other wounded men. But the last time he was not lucky. Twice wounded from the first rescues, he went down under a burst of machine gunfire as he was crawling back from the third man whose life he had saved.

Impressive, isn't it? Who can help but admire that heroic Jew?

72

Who would ever want to be tempted to play the coward after witnessing something like that? Who would not be made a better man by that example?

Well, that is part of the meaning of the Passion of Jesus. No one can look at Him as He approaches Calvary without wanting to be a better and more courageous person!

We see in Jesus not only a brave man, a holy man, a just man, but we see all of His bravery, all of His holiness, all of His goodness lifted up to the highest level we know in human life—the level of sacrificial love. It is this that we put at the heart of our religion.

Yet the Passion of Christ means even more than that. We Christians not only believe that Jesus was a man—we believe that He was God. Here is something immeasurably more significant. *The greatest meaning of the sacrifice of Jesus is that God loved us enough to suffer for us.* Sacrificial love is true not only on the level of human life; it is part of the very nature of God. It is the supreme essence of what God is.

Love does not fail at the top. If it were not so—

> The loving worm within its clod,
> Were diviner than a loveless god.
> —Robert Browning

Human love can strengthen and comfort us. Only belief in God's unfailing love can save us at times from despair. No matter what happens to us, this belief provides us with the power of ultimate hope for our salvation. The Cross with God pouring out His love upon it is something we can understand. That is why it was right for Christ to die.

The Cross is the highest symbol of our faith. It is woven into the clerical vestments. It is embroidered in the linen upon the altar. It is graven in our communion vessels. It is carried in procession. It is lifted high above the altar. It is signed upon our foreheads in baptism. It is made in sweeping gestures of blessing and absolution. It is the richest note in our hymnology. It is the center of our preaching. It is the very heart of the Gospel. It is the symbol of the everlasting Love of God.

73

14. The Facts of Easter

Recall the scene of the first Easter. As daylight began to break, three women came to the tomb where the body of Jesus had been placed. They had come to prepare his body for final burial. To their astonishment, the stone which sealed the tomb was rolled away. Sitting on the stone was an angel, whose "countenance was like lightning, and his raiment white as snow." The women were so frightened they could not speak.

> And the angel . . . said . . . Fear not ye: for I know that ye seek Jesus, which was crucified. He is not here: for he is risen, as he said. Come, see the place where the Lord lay. And go quickly and tell his disciples that he is risen from the dead . . . (Matt. 28:5-7) And as [the women] went . . . behold, Jesus met them, saying, All hail.
>
> (Matt. 28:9)

On Easter we celebrate the Resurrection of our Lord Jesus Christ. It is the greatest event in the history of the world! It is great because it demonstrated three facts of life.

The first fact is that Jesus Christ was the divine Son of God. If He had been merely another man, He would not have risen from the dead. It is not hard to grant that Jesus was one of the greatest men the world has ever seen. Anyone who becomes familiar with Christ's teachings will have to admit that He had authentic genius. If the world were to make up a list of the ten most important men of all time, Jesus Christ would surely appear as everybody's choice.

Yet it is one thing to be a genius. It is quite another to rise from the dead! Moses was a great genius, but when he died, he stayed dead. Plato had a brilliant mind, but he did not rise from the dead. St. Francis of Assisi is the world's most attractive saint. But we know only the memory of St. Francis' beautiful life. We do not worship him as a living God.

By the same token, if there had been no resurrection, someone might have remembered enough of Jesus' parables to write them down. But, there would be no Church today unless Christ had risen from the dead.

So here we have one of the most remarkable facts of human history. Christians gather on Easter, and on every other Sunday, not to honor a dead genius, but to witness to each other and to the world, nineteen hundred years after it happened, that the same Jesus whom men crucified rose from the dead and is now to be worshipped as the living God.

The second stupendous fact is this: Easter Day has demonstrated that life continues after death. The Resurrection of Jesus Christ is the one single historical fact which proves that life goes on beyond the grave. Life does not make sense unless we live again after physical death has overtaken us.

Before the first Easter Day, many generations of men instinctively knew that somehow the human soul survived death. There has never been a civilization that did not cling to the belief in some kind of afterlife. Not until the present age has any group of people lived without belief in life hereafter. Modern Communism is the only product of human thought which denies life after death.

Yet, in spite of a universal tendency of all mankind to believe in survival after death, the rising of Christ on Easter Day is the one and only demonstration in history that immortality is true. Life is no garden of roses for the majority of men. On the contrary, it is often a fearsome episode fraught with frightening difficulties. For most men it is an endless struggle to keep body and soul together. True, it offers moments of deep satisfaction and peace. Far more frequently it offers fear, uncertainty, and deep troubling of the spirit. Who is the man, who looking back can honestly say, I am satisfied with my life and I am ready now to have it end in death?

We may be weary of life. But we are rarely satisfied with it! We may welcome death as a respite for a tired and ailing body or a burdened soul, but we all still yearn to go on with life in a world far better than what we have known.

To all who have tasted of life's greatest joys and deepest sorrows, Easter comes and the risen Christ proclaims, ". . . be of good cheer; I have overcome the world" (John 16:33). ". . . because I live, ye shall live also" (John 14:19). It is a welcome message of hope in the midst of the dread realities of life!

The third fact of Easter Day is that the Resurrection of Jesus Christ created the Christian Church. It is true that Pentecost, or Whitsunday, is called "the birthday of the Church." This is so because the Holy Spirit descended upon the disciples on Pentecost. From Pentecost on, the early Church began to preach about Christ. Yet it was Easter Day that witnessed the earliest beginnings of the Christian Church.

Remember that the Crucifixion nearly destroyed the little band of twelve disciples. Judas Iscariot committed suicide. Every last man among the remaining eleven, with the exception of John the beloved disciple, scurried into hiding when Christ was arrested on Maundy Thursday night. John was the only disciple with courage enough to come to the Cross on Good Friday. If Christ had remained dead, the band of disciples would have quickly disintegrated.

Instead, the women who saw the angel at the tomb and met Jesus on the road searched the cellars and backrooms of Jerusalem until they found Peter and John. Neither one could believe his ears when he heard that Christ had risen from the dead. They hurried by alleyways to the garden where Jesus had been buried. They went into the tomb. They found nothing except the burial clothes still wound in spiral form where Jesus' body had lain. They also found the cloth which had been over His face. This was not cast aside, but neatly folded, lying in a place by itself.

Then Peter and John spent the rest of the day trying to find the other hidden disciples. By nightfall they had gotten word to every one except Thomas. He was too well hidden. Then when the ten disciples gathered together, Christ appeared in the room, even though the door was locked. The disciples thought they were seeing

76

a ghost. But He asked for food, and showed them that He was flesh and blood. He ate bread and drank wine before them.

Two things Christ requested of His disciples that first Sunday night. One, that they find Thomas. Two, that they go back to Galilee where He would meet them and give them further instructions. A few days later, when Thomas had at last been found, Jesus appeared again to His disciples. These early meetings in Jerusalem, and those that took place in Galilee during the following forty days until Ascension Day, were the days which started the life of the Christian Church on its way.

If there had been no Resurrection, there would have been no Church.

So Easter Day reminds us of these three great facts of life. First, that Jesus Christ is the Son of God. Second, that life goes on for each of us after death. Third, that only the Risen Christ could have rallied the disciples and given them the power to begin the life of the Church.

In view of all that Easter means, it is no wonder that we call this day the most glorious of all the Christian Year!

15. Jesus Christ is King Forever

In A. D. 155 a cruel massacre took place in the city of Smyrna in Asia Minor. In that massacre St. Polycarp, a leading theologian was killed. It was one of the darkest periods in the turbulent second century of the Christian era.

A few years later the Christian community of Smyrna wrote the history of that sad time. They dated it in a most unusual way. They wrote: "Statius Quadratus being proconsul, but Jesus Christ being King forever."

This is a good time in the world's history to be reminded that evil is always temporary. Decency and goodness never die. Khrushchev may be proconsul of half the earth. But Jesus Christ is King forever!

Ours is not an easy age in which to live. We feel ourselves caught up in a torrent of unbelievable events. Our sensibilities receive rude shocks. Let us take heart from our religion and the experience of the past. Let us try to see today what we can do to help us live through the tensions of these times.

First of all, we Christians need to be reminded that we always live in two worlds while we are on earth. One of these is the immediate world of our day-to-day activities. We have families to love and children to raise. We have work to do. We must clothe, and house, and feed ourselves. We must co-operate with other people. In this daily life there will be both satisfaction and irritation. We shall face problems and find much pleasure.

But this is not the only world we live in or look forward to! We also live in the equally real world of the kingdom of God. It exists here on earth within the life of the Church and in the hearts of all believers. It is the only real life which will continue after death.

When Khrushchev shouts his accusations and threats before the United Nations, it is sad to think that one man would so blatantly threaten the decency of the world. Yet he represents just a part of the material world in which we live. We might be reminded of the story about a Scotch preacher of long ago. He was telling his congregation about the Day of Judgment. He described the torments of evil men in hell. He said, "All of you will one day come before the Judgment Seat. Those who have defied God will on that day fall on their knees and cry, 'Dear Lord, I did not know, I did not know!' And the Lord in his infinite justice will look down at them, and say, 'Well, now you know!'" Someday this bullying tyrant will be judged by God. Then he too will know.

No matter how atheistic Communism denies the existence of God, God still exists. No matter how weak nations like Hungary or Tibet are crushed by the military might of Communism, God exists. No matter how evil men intrigue to establish their malignant control over free men, God exists. No tyranny has ever lasted long in history. Such men are merely proconsuls, who appear for a brief space in human affairs, and are destroyed by the ruthless force of their own ambitions or by the relentless passage of time. History is always under the control of God.

If man were destined only to live within the dimensions of his material, earthly life, evil might be able to place him in lasting bondage. But he lives in a spiritual realm as well. Here he is strengthened by his faith. Here flourish his dearest hopes and his ideals. Here he will ever find strength to strive for freedom. Here he is moved by loyalty to values which transcend all selfish interests.

Give thought in these times to this spiritual kingdom which is your true home. You will find great sources of strength here. You will find the detachment and calm we all need to live amidst the dangers of the present day.

How can the Christian religion help us when we are deeply concerned about our problems? One line in the third chapter of the Epistle to the Ephesians is especially important for the times we are going through: ". . . be strengthened with might by his Spirit in the inner man; That Christ may dwell in your hearts by faith . . ." (Eph. 3:16-17). Never in our lifetime was it so important to have faith. Every one of us who has lived through the dark days of the two world wars knows how much we have needed faith in God. I do not know what the years ahead will bring. But one thing we can be sure about! Those men and women who are not strengthened by God's Spirit in the inner man—those people who do not have faith dwelling in their hearts are going to have a hard time. Those who have faith will also have the victory!

Our Lord Christ always asked one question of people who came to Him for help. It did not make much difference what their problem was. He asked them, "Do you have faith?" If they had it, even though it might be as small as a mustard seed, Jesus was able to help them.

One thing should be said about "faith" if we are really to understand it. Faith is not quite the same thing as "belief." The difference between the two is the chief reason why some people get no help from their religion when they really need it. Belief is the mental acceptance of certain ideas. Faith is the ability to trust a person.

Here is an illustration. Democracy is a set of political ideas. Many people believe they are the best political ideas ever evolved by men. If, however, Democracy is going to work, we must not only believe in its ideas, we must have faith in the people who possess the power to make these ideas work.

Nearly all Americans believe in Democracy. Farmers, business-men, Catholics, Jews, Protestants, white and colored, in the United States share the same basic convictions about the way of life called Democracy. In an election year each individual American votes neither for nor against Democracy. He votes for the person, or col-lection of persons called a Party, which he has the greatest faith will make Democracy work. The Constitution is a creed. An elec-tion is an act of faith, not in a program, but in a person.

The same is true of the Christian religion. It has a set of clear-cut beliefs. The all-important Christian ideas are set down in the Creeds of the Church. Christians by the hundreds repeat them every Sunday. The Creeds and Doctrines are important intellectual statements. But they are not "faith."

Faith is our personal trust in God and His Son Jesus Christ. The measure of our faith is the degree of our willingness to trust God in the daily issues of our life. Christian faith is the measure of our trust that Jesus Christ is God revealed to men. Carry it one step further. Christian faith is the length we are capable of going in accepting other men as our brothers in the family of Christ.

This religious faith is conditioned by the ideas of the Christian Church. Yet the Articles of the Christian Faith as set down in the Creeds are not the same thing as our personal store of trust in God. It is only when Christ dwells in our hearts by faith that we have the important "pearl of great price" which will enable us to face the problems of our daily life with a calm and quiet mind.

It was this kind of faith that the Christians of Smyrna had in the second century when they wrote of the massacre which killed St. Polycarp and hundreds of others: "Statius Quadratus being pro-consul, but Jesus Christ being King forever."

This is the long view which we all need today. This is the kind of

Christian faith which never doubts for a moment, even though "the heathen so furiously rage together," that God will have His way.

We should always remember that history shows over and over that good always comes out of dark times.

Athens produced the most beautiful culture in the ancient world. When did it do it? It was during the very years when the existence of Athens was threatened by Sparta.

Every year, in a series of High Holy Days, the Jewish people remember their slavery and deliverance from Egypt. Out of two thousand years of persecution came the Ten Commandments, the Laws of Moses, the noblest messages of the Hebrew prophets. And we should be grateful to them too, because out of the long sufferings of the Jews came the Christian religion.

Everyone has heard of the Age of the Renaissance in Western Europe. In it art was reborn. The great continental universities flowered. The spirit of scientific discovery was first launched. But let us not forget that during the Renaissance, England and France fought the Hundred Years' War, and the Thirty Years' War took place in the Low Countries. Yet out of all this travail eventually came most of the finer things which started nineteenth century Europe and America on their way.

If we keep one thing in mind, it will help us. Mankind has gone through great troubles in the past. There have been many periods in history when no sunshine appeared to brighten the way to the future. Yet always mankind has survived to go on to greater things. There is no reason, if we have faith in God, to believe that it will be otherwise today. Statius Quadratus may have been proconsul in Smyrna in A. D. 155. But who speaks his name, or kneels before his altar, or prays in his name today?—But Jesus Christ, being King forever, is quite a different matter for us all!

16. The Works of the Ascended Christ

For ninety-two years, Trinity Church in New York has celebrated the great Church festival of Ascension Day with magnificent music and a most elaborate liturgy. It is a fitting celebration, because Christians rejoice on this day that Jesus, whom God sent humbly into the world, now has returned to heaven and is enthroned in glory at the right hand of the Father.

Some Christian people might conclude that the Ascended Christ, having finished His task on earth, has no further thing to do! It may come as a surprise to many to learn that the Church has always believed that the work of Christ did not end when He ascended into heaven.

What has Christ done since His Ascension and what will He continue to do until the Final Day of Judgment?

First, Christ now reigns over all creation. He is Christ the King. The earthly life of Jesus is so well known to us that we tend to think of Christ as He was on earth, rather than as He now is in His glory. It is true that in His resurrected body He bears forever the appearance of His Incarnation. The love for mankind is in His eyes. The nail prints of the Cross are visible in His hands. The scar made by the Roman soldier's spear is in His side.

Yet, He is not merely the kind and gracious Jesus of the Galilean hillside. He is the sovereign Lord who holds dominion over heaven, earth, and the entire cosmos. He is the Lord of life and death. He dwelleth in light unapproachable. Archangels and angels bow down before Him. The souls of the departed in Paradise adore Him and offer praise and thanksgiving to Him. His majesty is so great that we who are now alive cannot possibly picture it in our imagination.

The author of the Book of Revelation tried to describe it. You will recall St. John's famous words:

> After this I looked, and, behold, a door was opened in heaven: and the first voice which I heard was as it were of a trumpet talking with me; which said, Come up hither, and I will shew thee things which must be hereafter. And immediately I was in the spirit; and, behold, a throne was set in heaven, and one sat on the throne. And he that sat was to look upon like a jasper and a sardine stone: and there was a rainbow round about the throne, in sight like unto an emerald. And round about the throne were four and twenty seats: and upon the seats I saw four and twenty elders sitting, clothed in white raiment; and they had on their heads crowns of gold. And out of the throne proceeded lightnings and thunderings and voices: and there were seven lamps of fire burning before the throne, which are the seven Spirits of God. And before the throne there was a sea of glass like unto crystal: and in the midst of the throne, and round about the throne, were four beasts full of eyes before and behind. And the first beast was like a lion, and the second beast like a calf, and the third beast had a face as a man, and the fourth beast was like a flying eagle. And the four beasts had each of them six wings about him; and they were full of eyes within: and they rest not day and night, saying, Holy, holy, holy, Lord God Almighty, which was, and is, and is to come. And when those beasts give glory and honour and thanks to him that sat on the throne, who liveth for ever and ever, The four and twenty elders fall down before him that sat on the throne, and worship him that liveth for ever and ever, and cast their crowns before the throne, saying, Thou art worthy, O Lord, to receive glory and honour and power: for thou hast created all things, and for thy pleasure they are and were created.
>
> (Rev. 4)

This should be the picture in your mind when you think of Christ as He is today. Jesus of Nazareth died upon the Cross. Christ the King reigns eternally at the right hand of the Father.

The second work of the Ascended Christ is to intercede before

God the Father on our behalf and on behalf of the souls in Paradise. This is a sobering thought. At every moment of the day or night, Christ prays for the salvation of men. You and I, caught up as we are so frequently in a thousand concerns of daily life, often forget Jesus. It may even be that some of us have grown so careless that we have not worshipped Him regularly on Sunday, or even said our prayers. Yet, not for a single moment does Christ forget any one of us. Our every thought and deed are known to Him. When we do that which is right and charitable, Christ offers thanks on our behalf. When we are tempted to sin, He agonizes over our decision. When trouble comes upon us, He prays His Father that we be given strength to endure and emerge victorious.

The sacrifice which Jesus made upon the Cross is perpetually offered by the Ascended Christ for the salvation of our souls. If we remember this, we will not take Christ lightly at any time. This thought will help us to be faithful in regular worship. It will also remind us that, if Christ in heaven is praying for us, we ought also to pray for other people.

The third work of the Ascended Christ is to send the Holy Spirit to His followers. You will recall that, while Christ was yet alive before His crucifixion, He had said to His anxious disciples: "Nevertheless I tell you the truth; It is expedient for you that I go away: for if I go not away, the Comforter will not come unto you; but if I depart, I will send him unto you" (John 16:7).

The disciples did not understand the meaning of these words until the Day of Pentecost. We celebrate Pentecost as Whitsunday. It comes ten days after Ascension Day. As His followers were gathered together, "suddenly there came a sound from heaven as of a rushing mighty wind, and it filled all the house where they were sitting. And there appeared unto them cloven tongues like as of fire, and it sat upon each of them. And they were all filled with the Holy Ghost . . ." (Acts 2:2-4).

Ever since that day, the Church has felt the power of the Holy Spirit which the Ascended Christ has continued to send generation after generation upon His faithful people. He is given to every bishop when he is consecrated; the bishop gives the Holy Spirit to every clergyman he ordains, and to every child and adult whom he confirms.

Nor is the Holy Spirit confined to the Christian Church. He is at work in the lives of men whether they recognize it or not. He informs the mind. He guides humanity. He bends history inexorably in the direction of the will of God.

The uniqueness of the Christian Church lies not in its beliefs, but in the fact that it is the Spirit-filled community whose role it is to reveal God in Christ and convert the world.

The Nicene Creed sums up in remarkable brevity what we believe about the Holy Spirit:

> And I believe in the Holy Ghost, The Lord, and Giver of Life, Who proceedeth from the Father and the Son; Who with the Father and the Son together is worshipped and glorified; Who spake by the Prophets.

Whatever courage we possess, whatever patience we display, whatever love is in our hearts, whatever forgiveness we are capable of, whatever faith we have in God,—all this is the Holy Spirit at work in us. He was, and continues to be sent to us by the Ascended Christ.

Finally, Christ's last work will be to return to earth in glory and judge the quick and the dead. We should never be deceived into thinking that the Christian Church no longer believes in the final coming of Christ and the Day of Judgment. On the contrary, the Church believes that all creation is a temporary and passing thing. This includes the earth on which we live, and all the planets, stars and nebulae of matter in the cosmos. None of it is eternal. It had a beginning and it will have an end. That end could be today. It could be tomorrow. It may not occur for centuries. There is nothing sacred or eternal about the material universe. Only the Being of God, the existence of the Hosts of Heaven, and the souls of men are sacred and unending.

The real purpose of human life is to prepare for the Last Judgment and for life eternal. He who lives his life from day to day without concern for his final destiny does not truly believe in the

85

Christian God. In the Epistle to the Colossians, St. Paul wrote these words:

> If ye then be risen with Christ, seek those things which are above, where Christ sitteth on the right hand of God. Set your affection on things above, not on things on the earth. For ye are dead, and your life is hid with Christ in God. When Christ, who is our life, shall appear, then shall ye also appear with him in glory.
>
> (Col. 3:1-4)
>
> Put on therefore, as the elect of God, holy and beloved, bowels of mercies, kindness, humbleness of mind, meekness, longsuffering; Forbearing one another, and forgiving one another, if any man have a quarrel against any: even as Christ forgave you, so also do ye. And above all these things put on charity, which is the bond of perfectness. And let the peace of God rule in your hearts, to the which also ye are called in one body; and be ye thankful.
>
> (Col. 3:12-15)

The true Christian keeps his mind on "those things which are above" because he believes that this present life on earth is merely a brief preparation for eternal life.

Let us remember, especially during Ascensiontide, that God and His Beloved Son do not sit passively by. They are actively involved in human history and in the daily life of each one of us. Jesus said, "My Father worketh hitherto, and I work" (John 5:17).

St. Paul understood this well when he wrote, ". . . thanks be to God, which giveth us the victory through our Lord Jesus Christ. Therefore, my beloved brethren, be ye stedfast, unmoveable, always abounding in the work of the Lord, forasmuch as ye know that your labour is not in vain in the Lord" (I Cor. 15:57-8).

17. Christ's Second Coming

The early years of the Christian Church were years of severe suffering and persecution of Christians. As a result, the twelve apostles and their followers believed that in their lifetime Christ would return to earth and overthrow the powers of evil in one last glorious victory. This belief in the Immediate Second Coming prevailed for three hundred years. Some Christian groups, like the Seventh-Day Adventists and Jehovah's Witnesses, still cling to this so-called Messianic Hope, and make it the central theme of their religion today. Throughout history, whenever the nations have faced dreadful crises, the Second Coming and the end of the world have been prophesied. Today, threatened as we are by the holocaust of nuclear obliteration, it is not hard to understand the popularity of Billy Graham, who dwells upon the same theme.

This is not the belief, however, of the Episcopal Church, or, for that matter, of any other part of Catholic Christendom. We do not look forward to some dazzling moment when the end of the world will take place, and when Christ will appear on this earth to reward the good people and punish the bad people.

Rather, we believe that Christ comes to us daily in every single decision we make. Christ confronts every individual and every group on earth at every moment, with the simple question: "Is your act in conformity with My Gospel, or is it contrary to My Gospel?"

This is not to imply that the Church does not believe in a final judgment of each single person who was ever born. That will take place in the next life, after each of us has had a new oportunity in Paradise, where we need not battle against the temptations and limitations of our earthly bodies. The Final Judgment takes place at the end of our sojourn in Paradise, and will determine whether we are fit for eternal life in Heaven, or by our constant rebellion against God, are fit only to live in Hell.

In other words, while it is quite possible that mankind in his stupidity can wipe out all or nearly all of life on earth, if nuclear war were to start in our generation, the Church does not believe that Christ will at that dreadful moment appear to judge the quick and the dead. Nor do we believe that that would be the end of mankind. God will patiently start all over again on earth to re-create mankind. Nothing can thwart God's will. He can wait for centuries for humanity on this planet to accept His Gospel and live by it. Meanwhile, every human decision is being judged by that Gospel, whether Christ is believed in and accepted, or not.

In the light of this doctrine of the Church, we should not get overly worked up at the prospects of nuclear war. In many ways it is irrelevant to build a fall-out shelter. It does not matter in the least whether our bodies survive. What does matter is that our souls will survive. What matters is that, while we are here on earth, we ac-knowledge Christ to be the Incarnate Son of God. What matters is that we do our best each day to live in accordance with Christ's teaching and example. What matters is that we spend our lives making Christ known to as many other people as we can.

All other human activity—be it government, politics, ownership of wealth, management of industry, labor, art, scientific investiga-tion, education, medicine, the military, as important as each may seem to be—is, in the eyes of the Christian Church, secondary to the conversion of mankind to the Gospel of Christ.

So, let us be as clear as we can that the Anglican Communion does not believe in the end of the world or the Immediate Second Coming of Christ.

We believe that the Final Judgment comes at the end of each person's long sojourn in Paradise. In order to help people avoid fear of death, let us also be clear as to exactly what the Christian Church believes about the future life. We believe that when we die, our souls enter Paradise. This is true of every human soul. Paradise is the place where each of us has a second and final opportunity to achieve perfection. The Gospels do not tell us how long we shall dwell in Paradise. Probably there is no average span of life there. It is consistent with the mercy and patience of God, however, to assume that each soul will be given sufficient time there to grow Christlike.

Our religion also teaches us that each one of us possesses freedom of will. You and I have it here on earth, and we shall have it in Paradise. This means that each of us is free to obey God or rebel against Him. Jesus is the only Man who ever lived who obeyed God's will perfectly on earth. A few men and women since Christ's day came so close to perfect obedience in their earthly lives that the Church now calls them saints. All the rest of mankind is composed of a mixture of good and bad. None of these, and none of us are ready at death to enter God's Presence in Heaven. We all need a longer time than this life here provides to grow in saintly perfection. That is why God has provided, in His infinite mercy, an intermediate state between life on earth and Heaven. This intermediate state, where all souls go after the death of their bodies, is called Paradise.

The same freedom to obey God or to rebel against Him will be ours in Paradise, just as it is on earth. But there are three great differences in Paradise which help every soul strive toward perfection. The first is that we shall be freed of the limitations and temptations which attend our physical bodies while we are here on earth.

So many of our troubles on earth are caused by the weaknesses of our flesh. To feed our bodies, to clothe them, to make them comfortable, to give them rest, we struggle in competition with every other human being. When our bodies become ill, or as we gradually age, we try anxiously to protect ourselves. Our earthly bodies are both a source of joy and the cause of our most selfish temptations. At death the soul is separated from the body. The soul enters Paradise free at last of every concern which our body daily makes upon us. Thus free of the flesh in Paradise, we shall be able to concentrate more completely on spiritual values.

The second great advantage we shall have in Paradise is that we shall frequently see our Lord Christ there. He moves freely and often between Heaven and Paradise. This means that every soul will see more clearly the person and example of Jesus. With this greater clarity, each of us will get the inspiration and enthusiasm to strive to be like Him. St. Paul put it this way: "For now we see through a glass, darkly; but then face to face . . ." (I Cor. 13:12).

The third advantage of life in Paradise is that there we shall be reunited with our loved ones, and become acquainted with all of the great and growing souls who have gone before us. These, too, will be an encouragement and inspiration to us.

Yet, let us remember that in Paradise we shall still possess free will. We can choose to grow slowly toward perfection there, or we can turn our backs on God and continue to rebel against Him. Life in Paradise will not be easy. We shall not in a moment become perfect saints. We shall be tempted in Paradise. It is possible to sin in Paradise. But we shall not be tempted or sin because of our fleshly bodies.

What finally happens to the soul? Paradise is an intermediate state and the souls of the departed do not remain there indefinitely. The Church believes that after each soul has had sufficient time to achieve perfection, or to demonstrate its incorrigible rebellion against God, it comes before Christ for final judgment. This is the Judgment Day against which the Scriptures and the Prayer Book warn us. This is the moment which is spoken of in the marriage service, where it is called "the dreadful day of judgment when the secrets of all hearts shall be disclosed." At that Final Judgment, Christ will decide whether each one of us is fit to enter Heaven, where we shall see God face to face, or whether we are fit only for that state of eternal separation from God, and from all other souls, which is commonly referred to as Hell.

So, the Second Coming which the Church believes in is this coming of Christ at the end of our stay in Paradise—His coming to judge our ultimate destiny.

Therefore, in these perilous days, do not despair. Take heart from the knowledge that no act of mankind can permanently thwart God's will. Take heart from Christ's teaching that the little span of our earthly life is but a tiny part of our eternal existence. Let us live in the confidence of a sure and certain hope. Let us look at the future with the same triumphant outlook as the author of the Epistle to the Romans, when he said:

> Who shall separate us from the love of Christ? shall tribulation, or distress, or persecution, or famine, or nakedness, or peril, or sword? . . . Nay, in all these things we are more than conquerors through him that loved us. For I am persuaded, that neither death, nor life, nor angels, nor principalities, nor powers, nor things present, nor things to come, Nor height, nor depth, nor any other creature, shall be able to separate us from the love of God, which is in Christ Jesus our Lord.
>
> (Rom. 8:35-9)

III

GOD, THE HOLY GHOST

18. The Holy Spirit

Whitsunday is properly called the Festival of the Holy Spirit, because, on this day, the Christian Church commemorates that great event, which took place ten days after the Ascension of Christ, when God sent the Holy Ghost in power to the disciples. On that day the Christian Church was born.

What do Christians believe about the Holy Spirit? Church people have little difficulty understanding God as our heavenly Father. They also have a clear picture in their minds about Jesus, the incarnate Son of God. However, it is not so easy for us to visualize God the Holy Ghost.

To begin with, let us remember that, even though the Holy Spirit descended in power upon the disciples on the Day of Pentecost, this great gift of spiritual strength was not the beginning of the existence of the Holy Spirit. Just as Christ was with God the Father before He became a man, so also the Holy Ghost existed always.

If we examine the Old Testament carefully, we will find that the Holy Spirit is the power by which God acts. The Book of Genesis begins with these words: "In the beginning God created the heaven and the earth. And the earth was without form, and void; and darkness was upon the face of the deep. And the Spirit of God moved upon the face of the waters." This means that the Holy Spirit created all things.

In time all life, including human life, evolved as the result of the work of the Holy Spirit. Job says, "The spirit of God hath made me, and the breath of the Almighty hath given me life" (Job 33:4).

Moreover, throughout the long centuries of human history, it is the Holy Spirit which has given wisdom to mankind's greatest leaders. Isaiah, who towers above all the prophets of the Old Testament in his understanding of the needs of mankind, declared: "The Spirit of the Lord God is upon me; because the Lord hath anointed me to preach good tidings unto the meek; he hath sent me to bind up the brokenhearted, to proclaim liberty to the captives, and the opening of the prison to them that are bound" (Isaiah 61:1).

Yet, all through the Old Testament, the Holy Spirit acts only occasionally through certain men who give remarkable spiritual leadership to Israel. His power is not yet available to all men. The Old Testament ends with the longing for the time that is yet to come, when God will pour out His Holy Spirit on all people. In the Book of Joel there is the most famous expression of this late Old Testament hope: "And it shall come to pass afterward, that I will pour out my spirit upon all flesh; and your sons and your daughters shall prophesy, your old men shall dream dreams, your young men shall see visions" (Joel 2:28).

All this means that throughout all creation and the gradual evolution of life upon this earth, God acted by means of the Holy Spirit. Yet, the common man still needed a means of acquiring the tremendous power of God's spiritual strength. This was not to come until God sent His Son, Jesus Christ, into the world.

Of course, we all know that it is on this note of the imminent coming of such salvation that the New Testament begins. In the first chapter of St. Mark's Gospel, John the Baptist prophesied the coming of the Saviour in these words: "There cometh one mightier than I after me, the latchet of whose shoes I am not worthy to stoop down and unloose. I indeed have baptized you with water: but he shall baptize you with the Holy Ghost" (Mark 1:7-8).

One of the chief differences between the Old Testament and the New Testament is that in the New Testament *Jesus of Nazareth is described as the first man in all history to have possessed the Holy Spirit in all its fullness!* You all recall that when Jesus was baptized by John in the river Jordan, "the heavens opened, and [he saw] the Spirit like a dove descending upon him" (Mark 1:10). From that time until the Day of Pentecost, the Holy Spirit is united to the person of Jesus Christ! From that day, every word that Jesus spoke and every act that He performed reveal the power of the Holy Spirit.

We must always remember that the divinity of Christ does not rest upon His Virgin Birth! Nor does it rest upon His example and teaching! Neither does it rest upon His remarkable self-control and gentleness as He died upon the Cross! Nor does it rest upon His Resurrection! *The divinity of Christ rests first and last upon the fact that the Holy Spirit so completely engulfed Jesus that He always acted in perfect unity with the will of God the Father.*

Now we are ready to examine how the Holy Ghost has been made available to men since the Resurrection. Recall the Biblical description of the first Whitsunday: "And when the day of Pentecost was fully come, [the disciples] were all with one accord in one place. And suddenly there came a sound from heaven as of a rushing mighty wind, and it filled all the house where they were sitting. And there appeared unto them cloven tongues like as of fire, and it sat upon each of them. And they were all filled with the Holy Ghost, and began to speak with other tongues, as the Spirit gave them utterance" (Acts 2:1-4).

So filled were the disciples with this wonderful new spiritual power that they ran out into the streets. Immediately a crowd gathered. Some bystanders thought that the disciples had gotten drunk.

Finally, St. Peter quieted everybody down. Then he explained what had happened: "Ye men of Israel, hear these words; Jesus of Nazareth, a man approved of God among you by miracles and wonders and signs . . . Him . . . ye have . . . crucified and slain: Whom God hath raised up, having loosed the pains of death . . . having received of the Father the promise of the Holy Ghost, he [Christ] hath shed forth this [same Holy Spirit], which ye now see and hear . . . Repent, and be baptized every one of you in the name of Jesus Christ . . . and ye shall receive the gift of the Holy Ghost. For the promise is unto you, and to your children, and to all that are afar off . . . Then they that gladly received his word were baptized: and the same day there were added unto them about three thousand souls" (Acts 2:22-41).

Thus, having received the power of the Holy Spirit, the Christian Church was born! We all know the rest of the story. On fire with zeal and faith, the twelve apostles within their lifetime spread the Gospel of Christ to every part of the Roman Empire. So it has been in every age since then. The Holy Spirit has found men and women in each generation, including the present, who have devoted their lives to Christ and His Church. It is through the Church that the Holy Spirit is available to each one of us today.

It is the Holy Spirit who makes the Church increase. It is the Holy Spirit who inspires the decisions which result in the work the Church does. It is the Holy Spirit which has provided purpose and meaning to the lives of millions of men and women. It is the Holy Spirit which inspires the high ideals of love and sacrifice by which the Church at its best has always lived. It is the Holy Ghost who comforts and sustains each of us by Word and Sacrament in the difficult crises of life. It is by the power of the Holy Spirit that we shall pass through the gates of death and rise triumphant as did Christ.

How do we receive the Holy Spirit? It is not given to every man or woman! We receive the Holy Spirit when we are baptized. It is strengthened and confirmed in us when the bishop lays his hand upon us at our confirmation. It is renewed each time we receive Holy Communion. Thus, through the ongoing Church, we today receive the cleansing, strengthening power of the Holy Spirit of God.

As we go through life, we need many things. We need good parents. We need an education. We need opportunity to do satisfying work. We need nourishment and rest. We need enough money to retain human dignity. We need friends. We need ideals, high hopes, and inspiring examples of other people. Yet, we need one thing for our salvation more than we need any of these other things. We need above everything else the power of the Holy Spirit. For this cause God sent His only begotten Son into the world. Through Christ, the Holy Ghost takes possession of us.

It is a mistake to assume that the Holy Spirit of God automatically will grow strong in our lives simply because we have been baptized and confirmed. Each of us must first surrender our will to God's will. Each of us must be faithful in prayer, regular in communion, strong in self-discipline, and willing to serve our fellow men. Religion is something which God does with us. It is never that which we do for God.

19. The Power of the Holy Spirit

There is hardly a page of the New Testament which does not speak about the Holy Ghost. When St. Luke described the Annunciation, he wrote: ". . . the angel . . . said unto [Mary], The Holy Ghost shall come upon thee . . . therefore also that holy thing which shall be born of thee shall be called the Son of God" (Luke 1:35). At the baptism of Jesus "the Holy Ghost descended . . . like a dove upon him" (Luke 3:22). Again the Holy Ghost is spoken of as the power which drove Jesus to face his temptation in the wilderness. Finally, in the closing passage of St. Matthew's Gospel, the divinity of the Holy Ghost is taught: "Go ye therefore, and teach all nations, baptizing them in the name of the Father, and of the Son, and of the Holy Ghost" (Matt. 28:19).

Why is belief in the reality of the Holy Spirit so prominent in the New Testament? And why is it important to us?

It is obvious that possession of the Holy Spirit gave the early Christians power to stand strong against a hostile Roman Empire. The society into which the Christian Church was born was ruthless and materialistic. In it the upper classes conspired to gain power and wealth. There was no strong religion able to inspire true morality. It was an age of growing cynicism. For a large part of the population, life was filled with futility. The virtues of hope, discipline, sacrifice, courage, and integrity were growing weaker. Life became frustrating for the masses. The purposes for which men strove seemed increasingly meaningless and hollow.

Into this declining culture came the Christian Church. Its members had experienced an outpouring of power from God. As a result, Christians saw life in a new and invigorating framework. They looked into the future with unshakable faith because of the Risen Christ. The Holy Spirit saved them from despair, and it brought them a new, galvanizing will to action. They were flooded with an enthusiasm which was new to each of them, and which was lacking in those who were not Christians.

This morale-building power of the Holy Spirit proved to be the spiritual dynamic which created a new society out of the ancient Roman world. Because the early Christians felt this new Holy Spirit so strongly, it is prominent in all of the New Testament writings.

What about ourselves and the times in which we live? It is not easy for any of us to realize how much has happened to the world in our lifetime. We have lived through two world wars. It staggers the imagination to picture what it means to go, in one generation, from the slow pace of the early part of this century to the missile age. While we have been adjusting to fantastic scientific progress, the monstrous darkness of Communism has blotted out freedom for half the population of the earth. It casts its grim shadow on us all.

Ours is very much like the age in which the Christian Church was born. It is an age of deep anxiety and danger. Yet, like the early Christian era, the only men who have the spiritual capacity to save civilization are those who are moved by the Holy Spirit of God. The new paganism of the present day is very strong. Yet it is materialistic and capable of inhumanity beyond belief. But never in history have cynical, godless men been able to build the foundation of a society that will endure. They possess no image of a God of goodness. They are restrained by no moral principle except expediency. They have no loyalty except to naked power. The spirit which motivates them is an evil spirit. It is an idol with feet of clay.

There is no great secret about the meaning of the Holy Ghost.

It is one of the most basic ideas in the Christian religion. The Holy Ghost is the gift of spiritual power which makes it possible for those who possess it to win and transform the world. It was given to the Church on the first Whitsunday. It is to be found within the fellowship of the Church today. In some measure, small or great, it is in each one of us. The stronger our faith is, the stronger it will grow in us. Nothing else will bring us peace. No other power save that of the Holy Spirit of God can save the world.

20. The Fruit of the Spirit

Of all the creatures God has made, we men are not completely at home here on this earth. Unlike animals, it is not enough for us to feed our bodies, protect ourselves from weather, and reproduce our kind. We have all the physical desires of an animal. But we also are aware that there is a difference between good and evil. We are insatiably curious about our past and our future. We believe that life has eternal meaning. We yearn to love and be loved. We cannot endure the notion that death is the end. We work hard to earn a living, all the while knowing that merely to earn a living is not enough. We want to live without fear. We want to give ourselves to a worthwhile cause that is bigger than our little lives. We need dignity and peace of mind as much as we need food and clothing.

All of this has been true of man for centuries. It is still true today. Consequently, St. Paul was accurately describing human life when he wrote: "For the flesh lusteth against the Spirit, and the Spirit [struggles] against the flesh: and these are contrary the one to the other . . ." (Gal. 5:17).

All of us are only too familiar with the works of the flesh, and we know that what St. Paul has to say about them is only too true. But let us focus our attention on his description of what he calls "the fruit of the Spirit."

It is always easier to remember what these spiritual virtues are if we divide them into three groups. St. Paul lists nine fruits of the Spirit. The first three have to do with our relationship to God. These are love, joy and peace. The next three describe how we should treat our neighbors. They are longsuffering, gentleness and goodness. And the last three describe the virtues each one of us should have in our personal devotional lives. They are faith, meekness and temperance.

Let us look briefly at each one.

First there is love. Have you ever asked yourself why God created mankind? He could have stopped when He created the planets and the distant stars. He could have stopped when He created the animals of this earth. Apparently man was created because God wanted an intelligent creature capable of knowing that God exists, and capable of loving God as God loves His creation. The planets and stars cannot love God. Animals cannot love God. Man is the only living creature on this earth who is able to return God's love. This is what Jesus was saying in the wonderful parable of the Prodigal Son. The son, in his final misery, turned homeward to seek his father. And the father welcomed him with joy because he really needed and wanted his lost son's love. Love of God for each human being and the act of loving God in return is the cornerstone of the Christian religion.

Out of this mutual love of God and man always comes true joy. We modern people spend a lot of time and money seeking happiness. Rarely does one ever hear the word joy used. Yet joy is one of the nine fruits of the Spirit. Happiness is not even mentioned. The distinction between happiness and joy is simply this. Happiness is a temporary condition usually connected with a pleasant event which quickly passes. Joy, when finally found, endures for life. A man and woman are happy on their wedding day. If their marriage is a good and lasting one, it gradually brings them joy. Joy is a quiet, enduring virtue. It is this joy which slowly develops in our hearts as we love God and know ourselves loved by Him through the good and bad of life.

The third fruit of the Spirit is peace. Christian peace is not to be confused with the passive enjoyment of freedom from strife and daily troubles. Rather, it means the calm confidence which comes from knowing that God exists; that He truly loves each of us; and that regardless of what life brings, nothing can separate us now or eternally from our heavenly Father's love. Peace is the absolute belief that God can be trusted, and that we need have no enduring anxiety about anything.

These first three virtues—love, joy and peace—are all fruits of our relationship with God.

The next three fruits of the Spirit are the virtues we need to live with other people. To repeat, they are longsuffering, gentleness and goodness.

Longsuffering is a very descriptive word for the Christian virtue of patience. It means that we try, with the grace of God's Holy Spirit, not to be short-tempered. Every man on earth has his shortcomings. In this earthly life, nobody, except our Lord Christ, is perfect. We live at a time in history which places high value on efficiency, industriousness, and accuracy. As a result, we not only do not suffer fools gladly, we are easily irritated when the smallest things go wrong. As Christians, our real vocation is to bear with the weaknesses of other people. Longsuffering is not to be confused with a spiritless good nature. It is patience with a purpose. The purpose of Christian longsuffering is to win, by example and forgiveness, the careless, the slothful, and the wayward to repentance and a better way of life. One of the best ways to cultivate the virtue of longsuffering is to remember daily how much God puts up with from each one of us.

Gentleness is the second virtue we need to live with other people. Very few faults are ever cured by a loud voice and an angry dressing-down. We do not like it when anyone tells us off in sharp tones. We and other people always respond better if we are corrected in a kindly but firm way. To be gentle does not mean to be wishy-washy. It means being capable of controlling anger. It means having respect for other people as human beings, who need desperately to maintain their sense of dignity.

The third virtue we need to live with other people is goodness.

This means being just in our dealings with other men. Nowadays the word "righteousness" has somehow taken on an unpleasant meaning. I think this is too bad. Because a truly righteous man is both a just and a good man. A good man tries to be fair and impartial in his treatment of people. He has a recognized high set of values by which he regulates his conduct.

These three virtues—longsuffering, gentleness and goodness—are indispensable in a Christian's relationships with other people.

Finally, we come to the last group of three which describe the chief characteristics of a Christian's inner life. They are faith, meekness and temperance. A Christian is a man who has a living faith in God and who has been baptized into the Church. He is one who is faithful in his practice of his religion. He not only believes with his mind, he does what his religion requires of him. You cannot have real faith without at the same time demonstrating your faithfulness. Faith in God always demands action. Do we worship regularly? If not, we had better ask ourselves if we really have faith in God. Do we pray, work and give for the spread of Christ's kingdom? If not, remember that faith without works is nothing.

The second virtue we need for our inner lives St. Paul calls "meekness." Unfortunately, this word too today has taken on an unpleasant shade of meaning. True meekness does not mean one is tame of spirit or disgustingly submissive. It means having an honest understanding of what we are really like. It is the opposite of haughty, boastful, and vain. It means the capacity to say, "I am not a god, but merely a man." Only the truly meek are able to repent themselves honestly of their sins and ask the forgiveness of God. That is why Christ in the Beatitudes said, "The meek shall inherit the earth." History has already demonstrated in Caesar, Napoleon and Hitler that the arrogant and proud inherit only violence, exile or death. As Christians, let us cultivate the virtue of true meekness.

The last virtue is temperance. This does not mean merely abstinence from alcoholic drinks. It means the capacity for "self-control" in all things. St. Paul had a measuring stick for giving rein to any desire or action. He subjected everything to two tests. He asked, "Is it helpful to other people; and is it to the glory of God?" If it was neither of these two things, he was then self-controlled about what he did. You and I should have the same temperance in all things.

These nine virtues are the Christian fruits of the Holy Spirit. For living with God: love, joy and peace are required. For living with other people: longsuffering, gentleness and goodness are required. For living with yourself: faith, meekness and temperance are required.

This is a strenuous set of virtues to develop. They only come with the growth of God's Holy Spirit in our lives. How strong they are in each one of us determines how much of a Christian each of us really is.

IV

THE CHURCH, THE BIBLE, THE SACRAMENTS

21. One Flock and One Shepherd

Many sincere people today are disturbed by the divisions within Christianity. They would like all Christians to belong to one great church. Usually they appeal to two authorities to prove that there should be only one church. They appeal first to the early history of Christianity. Then they point out the obvious waste and sin that exists when different Christian groups duplicate effort and compete with each other.

It is not very realistic to expect that, on so important a subject as religion, all men, at all times, everywhere, can be rigidly frozen into an unchanging ecclesiastical pattern. There is waste in the competition between denominations. It is the price free men must always pay to enjoy their freedom. It is to be preferred to the spiritual rigor mortis that inevitably follows when unbending conformity of the human spirit is enforced. Our Lord said, ". . . So there shall be one flock, one shepherd" (John 10:16 RSV). He did not say that there should be "one fold and one shepherd." In a flock there are many folds. And in the Christian fellowship there are many kinds of Christians. While we may personally prefer the Episcopal Church to any other, we should be quite ready to admit the right of someone else to prefer some other fold of his own choosing. We should expect to defend our religious preference vigorously. Therefore, we would not think highly of anyone who held a different point of view, if he did not do the same.

Let us look for a moment at the make-up of the whole group of Christian Churches. They are not nearly as divided as they seem. Most Christians belong to one of three great folds. The first group can be called the churches of the Ancient Catholic and Apostolic

Church. Together they are the most numerous Christians of the world. All of them are of a tradition of very early origin whose roots go back to the first centuries of the Christian era. They all possess the Apostolic ministry of bishops, priests and deacons. In all of them the Eucharist, or Holy Communion, is the central act of worship. All believe and use the same creed.

This first group includes the churches of the Eastern Episcopate. Many of them have dioceses in America. They are the following: the Ecumenical Patriarchate of Constantinople, the Patriarchate of Alexandria, the Patriarchate of Antioch, the Patriarchate of Jerusalem, the Patriarchate of Russia, the Patriarchate of Serbia (Yugoslavia), the Patriarchate of Romania, the Patriarchate of Bulgaria, the Church of Albania, the Church of Cyprus, the Church of Czechoslovakia, the Church of Finland, the Church of Georgia, the Church of Greece, the Church of Poland, the Church of Sinai, the Armenian Apostolic Church, the Coptic Church of Egypt, the Ethiopian Church, and the Syrian (Jacobite) Church. In this same family is the Church of the Old Catholic Episcopate.

Closely related to the ancient churches of the East and the Old Catholics is the Anglican Communion. The Episcopal Church in this country is an important part of this Anglican group.

A second family of churches were the product of the sixteenth century Reformation. The largest of these are: the Baptist Churches, the Lutheran Churches, the Methodist Churches, the Presbyterian Churches, the Congregational Churches, and the Evangelical Reformed Churches.

All of these denominations have repudiated the Apostolic Succession, the threefold order of the ministry, the central importance of Holy Communion as the norm of Sunday worship, and the historic creeds.

Still no one can deny that God's Holy Spirit has been at work among them. Today they feel most desperately the brokenness of the Christian fellowship. Through the World Council of Churches and the National Council of Churches of Christ in the U.S.A., they and many of the ancient apostolic churches are searching for ways of understanding each other and working together for the common good of mankind.

The third large group of Christians is the Roman Catholic Church. In its present form, it is a product of the Fourth Lateran Council in the thirteenth century. More particularly, it is the product of the Council of Trent, which was convened late in the sixteenth century to pull together the shattered remains of the medieval Papal Church which was badly disorganized by the Protestant Reformation.

Many of us cannot walk the way of the Protestant denominations because they repudiate the Apostolic Sacraments and discount the historic faith of Catholic Christendom. Nor is it possible for us to accept the exaggerated claims of the Papal Church to be the exclusive Body of Christ on earth. Both the Protestant denominations and the Roman Catholic Church have impressive accomplishments to their credit. We should hold their right to their convictions in the highest respect. We should be thankful that we live in a nation where men are free to differ about their religious affiliations and still esteem each other as human beings and as citizens of a free country. We should live up to our own ideals in such a way that other people will have respect for us.

If the Christian fellowship today is one flock made up of many folds, what is the prospect for the future? Will there one day come into existence one great united Church? No man has the wisdom to prophesy what will exist even a few decades hence. It does not seem possible that it is the will of God that the Church on earth shall always remain a flock separated into many folds. We should constantly pray and work for the unity of God's people.

In our Prayer Book on page 37 there is a remarkable prayer for unity:

> O God, the Father of our Lord Jesus Christ, our only Saviour, the Prince of Peace; Give us grace seriously to lay to heart the great dangers we are in by our unhappy divisions. Take away all hatred and prejudice, and whatsoever else may hinder us from godly union and concord: that as there is but one Body and one Spirit, and one hope of our calling, one Lord, one Faith, one

111

Baptism, one God and Father of us all, so we may be all of one heart and of one soul, united in one holy bond of truth and peace, of faith and charity, and may with one mind and one mouth glorify thee; through Jesus Christ our Lord. Amen.

Let each one of us first be sure he knows what his own church believes and requires of him. Let us strive to be better members of our own fold as the first step. Meanwhile respect the convictions of other Christians who are not Episcopalians. Then let us work as God gives us the opportunity to do so for better understanding and closer co-operation with other Christian Churches. Let us avoid reckless speed on the path to organic union; but let us also try to keep an open mind and a lively Christian hope for the growing unity of Christ's Body, remembering that with God all things are possible.

22. The Anglican Communion

On October 11, 1962, our separated brethren of the Roman Catholic Church began the Second Vatican Council. Christians throughout the world are deeply interested in this Council. We in the American Episcopal Church have asked God's blessing on the work of this Council and pray that the Holy Spirit will guide those who participate in it.

In the summer of 1963 the Second Anglican Congress took place in Toronto, Canada. To this came approximately four hundred bishops of our branch of the Holy, Catholic and Apostolic Church, many prelates who govern churches closely associated with us, and delegations of priests and lay people from the nearly 350 dioceses of the Anglican Communion around the world.

It, therefore, seems appropriate to consider what is the Anglican Communion.

Let me begin with a brief history of our world-wide Church.

As early as the second century of the Christian era, missionaries from Gaul in Western Europe came to the slowly dying cities of the Roman Empire in the British Isles. They made converts among soldiers of the Roman Legions and among the native barbarian peoples. Thus, the Christian Church in England is very old.

As the Roman Empire fell to pieces in the next three centuries, these early Christians of England lost contact with the growing dioceses of present-day France and Germany, and also with the Western center of Christianity, the City of Rome.

So it was that the Bishop of Rome, Gregory the First, in 597, not realizing that there were Christians in England, sent a band of missionary monks under the leadership of Augustine to evangelize the British Isles. To Augustine's astonishment, he was graciously received by King Ethelbert of Kent, whose wife Bertha was a Christian. The King was baptized on Whitsunday of that year, and on Christmas Day ten thousand of his Kentish subjects followed the King's example. As a result, Augustine was consecrated as the first Archbishop of Canterbury. The one-hundredth successor in this direct line of episcopal descent is the present Archbishop, the Most Rev. Arthur Michael Ramsey.

So, while there were many Christians in the British Isles from the earliest years of Christianity, the Anglican Communion began with St. Augustine in 597.

Augustine died in 604 and never succeeded in evangelizing England beyond Canterbury in his lifetime. Actually, it was not until the Council of Whitby in 664 that the ill-feeling, which he created with earlier Christian groups in other parts of England, ended. It was at Whitby that all English Christians agreed to associate with Canterbury. In the Middle Ages Papal primacy extended its feudal supremacy to all of Western Europe, including England. This association ended in the sixteenth century when the feudal system in Western Europe broke down and the Catholic Church in the British Isles separated itself from the exasperating domination of the Pope in Rome.

Today the Church of England is the established Church. This is no longer so in Wales, Ireland or Scotland. In 1920 the Welsh church was set apart and now contains six dioceses. In 1870 the Anglican Church of Ireland was made autonomous and has fourteen dioceses. In Scotland there are seven autonomous Anglican dioceses which have lived on good terms with the established Presbyterian Church since the seventeenth century.

The oldest Anglican churches outside the British Isles are the Episcopal Church in the United States and the Anglican Church of Canada. Trinity Church, New York, was one of the very earliest to be started in the American Colonies, and dates back to 1697. Trinity also played a role in the birth of the Canadian Church. The first Bishop of the Anglican Church in Canada had been Rector of this Parish. His name was Charles Inglis. He was a Tory during the American Revolution, as were most of the Vestry and many members. At the end of the Revolution, Dr. Inglis with others of his flock were exiled to Nova Scotia. From there this hardy man started the Anglican evangelization of Canada.

The Episcopal Church in the United States was formally organized in 1786. Today the Episcopal Church in the United States has 106 dioceses and missionary districts, including Alaska, Honolulu, Philippine Islands, Taiwan (Formosa), Mexico, Brazil, Liberia, and many others.

Out of Dr. Inglis' remarkable zeal, four provinces developed in nineteenth century Canada. In 1893 these separate provinces of the Anglican Communion united to form the Anglican Church of Canada. Today there are twenty-eight dioceses in the Canadian Church.

In more recent years the Anglican Communion has literally encircled the earth. Some dioceses were begun by English colonists. Such is the autonomous Church of England in Australia and Tasmania, and the Church of the Province of New Zealand. There are twenty-five dioceses in the Australian Anglican Church and nine in New Zealand.

Apart from these, all the other parts of the Anglican Communion were started by missionaries sent out from England, the United States, Canada, and Australia. Today in Japan and China our Anglican brothers are called the "Nippon Seikokai" (Japanese) and the "Chung Hua Sheng Kung Hui" (Chinese). In both languages the meaning of the name is the same: "The Holy Catholic Church in Japan" and "The Holy Catholic Church in China."

During the Second World War the Japanese Anglican Church suffered severe persecution. Many of its bishops and clergy went to jail. During the heavy bombing of Japanese cities, great destruction befell the churches. Today the Nippon Seikokai is strong and highly respected. There are ten dioceses in the Nippon Seikokai.

When China fell to the Communists, the Chinese Anglican Church was officially cut off from contact with the rest of the free world. At that time it had developed fourteen dioceses. No one knows exactly how the clergy and lay people of the Holy Catholic Church in China are getting along today. However, Christianity has always thrived on persecution. Chinese refugees who enter Hong Kong occasionally bring word about its plight. One thing is sure. The Holy Catholic Church of China is still alive. Its members need our daily prayers.

Missionaries from England brought the Church of England to India, Pakistan and Southeast Asia. Today the official name of the Anglican Communion in this area is "The Church of India, Pakistan, Burma and Ceylon." This autonomous Church is made up of sixteen dioceses.

Missionaries from England and the United States started the Anglican Communion in Africa. Liberia is still a missionary district of the Episcopal Church in our country. I believe that the Episcopal Church should quickly relinquish its jurisdiction there. Liberia ought to be speedily incorporated into one of the five autonomous Provinces of the Anglican Communion in Africa.

These five separate parts of the Anglican Communion in Africa are the following: The Church of the Provinces of Central Africa, West Africa, East Africa, Uganda and Ruanda-Urundi, and South Africa. We should be familiar with this area because Africa will probably be the most promising country in the world for the missionary work of the Anglican Church in the next twenty-five years.

In the British West Indies the Church of England has an autonomous Province. Here again, vast changes are underway. The missionary districts of the American Episcopal Church in Cuba, Puerto Rico, Haiti, the Dominican Republic, Central America, the Virgin Islands and the Panama Canal Zone should in time be united to the Anglican Church in the Province of the West Indies, which today includes Guiana, Antigua, Barbados, British Honduras, Jamaica, Nassau and the Bahamas, Trinidad, and the Windward Islands. When that happens, the Church in this area will be a single, autonomous Province.

The last autonomous member of the Anglican Communion is the Jurisdiction of the Archbishop of Jerusalem. Under his direction the dioceses of Jerusalem; Egypt and Libya; Iran; Jordan, Lebanon and Syria; and the Sudan are capably administered.

There are a few Anglican dioceses in South America but they are not yet an autonomous Province. These are directly responsible to the Archbishop of Canterbury.

In addition, there are nine dioceses which do not belong to any of the eighteen independent sections of the Anglican Communion. Each of these is directly administered under the guidance of the Archbishop of Canterbury. They are the dioceses of Argentina and Eastern South America with the Falkland Islands, Bermuda, Korea, Borneo, Singapore and Malaya, Madagascar, Mauritius, Gibraltar, and North Africa.

There are three dioceses in Brazil which were started by the American Episcopal Church, and still associated with it. These three are very close to becoming an independent section of the Anglican Communion.

Thus there are eighteen areas of the world in which independent parts of the Anglican Communion exist. In these eighteen lands there are 343 dioceses with a total membership of forty-three million baptized Christians. All of these independent churches are in communion with the original See of Canterbury and the Archbishop of Canterbury is the symbol of their unity.

Each of the eighteen parts of the Anglican Communion governs, finances and manages its own affairs. We do not have a central administrative bureau, such as the Roman Catholic Church has

116

in its Curia in the Vatican. In 1958 the Anglican bishops meeting at Lambeth decided that the Anglican Communion needed a central administrative officer to act as a liaison between the Archbishop of Canterbury and its eighteen autonomous sections around the world. An American bishop, the Rt. Rev. Stephen F. Bayne, Jr., now holds that office. He has accomplished much in his world-wide travels to strengthen the day-to-day ties between all parts of the Anglican Church.

Finally, we should note that the Anglican Churches are in full communion with many other Christian Churches. Among these are the Polish National Church in America, the Philippine Independent Church, the Old Catholic Churches of Europe, the Spanish Reformed Church, and the Lusitanian Catholic Church of Portugal. The Archbishop of Canterbury is working diligently to pave the way for full communion with the Eastern Orthodox Churches. We should pray that this will take place in the near future.

Much about our future relations with the Roman Catholic Church will depend on the decisions made in the Vatican Council now in session. We cannot expect quick reunion. However, if the bishops now assembled in Rome agree only to study and discuss the differences which now separate us, surely the Holy Spirit will guide their part of the Holy Catholic and Apostolic Church and ours toward unity.

Anglicans already co-operate and talk with many other Christians in the World Council of Churches. Full communion does not exist between most of them and us. Yet, leaders are getting to know each other. Unseemly competition is lessening among them. Relief work for the world's needy is steadily growing as a co-operative interchurch responsibility.

So, each of us should come to know what the Anglican Communion is, and to work and pray that the disputes and cleavages of earlier centuries may be lessened by a charitable and open-minded attitude, and that the present-day yearning for unity among all Christians may be set forward in our lifetime.

23. Episcopalians and the Bible

A few years ago an able and attractive evangelist spoke to thousands in Madison Square Garden. He is the most famous fundamentalist of our day. To him the Bible is in every word literally true. He drove his message home by repeating again and again, "The Bible says . . ." On the one hand, he strengthened the faith of many; on the other, he outraged scores who are well informed about the Scriptures.

What does the Episcopal Church believe about the Bible?

The simplest answer to this question is that in religion and in morals the Bible speaks the final word. The fact that the Bible was divinely inspired did not, however, prevent its writers from making mistakes about cosmogony, history, or science.

Nevertheless, with all its mistakes in these fields, it describes with remarkable accuracy what God is like. It proclaims truly what God has done.

We believe that the Old Testament traces the long, developing recognition by man of God's real nature. The New Testament proclaims with historic accuracy that God became a man in Jesus Christ. In the life and death of Christ is the only true demonstration of what each man can be. In the Gospels we see what God has done to make a great destiny possible for all who believe and follow Him.

We freely admit that much of the Old Testament reflects the limited knowledge of a primitive people. We accept the fact that the story of creation is Jewish mythology. We are not at all embarrassed by the crude tribal taboos reflected in Exodus and Leviticus. It delights us to recognize that the Song of Solomon and the Book of Psalms are lovely poetry. We are not in the least disturbed that the fable of Jonah and the Whale is an apocalyptic allegory, never intended to be taken literally. Long gone is the day when

Anglicans shivered at early archaeological discoveries that appeared to discredit the chronology of the Bible. Instead of denying all that modern scholarship has taught us about the Bible, the Episcopal Church has produced a number of the greatest Biblical scholars of all time. We should be proud that clergy like Burton Scott Easton, Frederick C. Grant, and Robert C. Dentan have been and are members of our Church. They and many others, who long ago dropped the fundamentalist point of view, made it possible for us to understand the Bible for what it gloriously is. It is not a literally accurate record of history or science. It is the world's most magnificent account of God acting savingly on behalf of man.

If this Anglican way of looking at the Bible does not rest its authority on the easy phrase of the fundamentalist, "the Bible says," on what does it rest its claim that the Holy Scripture is an authority for life?

Our claim rests upon three foundations. They are God, the Church, and a great vision. In the Bible, God speaks to man. Here He gradually reveals Himself. The revelation is dim in the early stages, but as we come to the prophets, it begins to brighten, until at last in the Gospels we see the full light of truth in Christ.

The second element in the authority of the Bible is contributed by the Church. The Books of the New Testament were written within the life of the Church. The Christian Church accepted the Old Testament of the Jews, and added to it the Books of the New Testament. The Church authorized the Bible. The Bible vindicates the Church. Therefore, part of the authority of the Bible is derived from the Church, which was God's instrument in producing it and making known its proclamation.

Its third source of authority is that it is the source of the most glorious vision man has ever had of what he is and what his destiny can be. It is a vision of "a new heaven and a new earth," of "a kingdom not made with hands," which has inspired and empowered Christians for two thousand years.

> [They] saw a new heaven and a new earth . . . [They] saw the holy city, new Jerusalem, coming down from God out of heaven, prepared as a bride adorned for her husband. [They]

heard a great voice out of heaven saying, Behold, the tabernacle of God is with men, and he will dwell with them, and they shall be his people . . . And God shall wipe away all tears from their eyes; and there shall be no more death, neither sorrow, nor crying, neither shall there be any more pain: for the former things are passed away. And he that sat upon the throne said, Behold, I make all things new.

(Rev. 21:1-5)

This is the Christian hope. It is this vision which drove Peter, John, Barnabas, and Paul out into a hostile Roman world. It is this hope which the Fathers of the Church saw all through the days of Imperial Roman persecution. It was this which inspired the building of the great Gothic churches with their arches leaping heavenward. It is this same vision of what life should and can be that has produced the saints and martyrs of all the generations. It is still this belief in the divine destiny of man that fans the faith of Christian men today.

Consider what the Bible is. It is the drama of man and God. It has for its stage the whole universe. It has for its plot the divine providence. It has for its period all time. It has for its hero a loving Father. The prologue to the drama begins with the majestic sweep of creation. The plot begins when Abraham appears on history's stage seeking "a city which hath foundations, whose builder and maker is God" (Heb. 11:10). Then it sweeps through the cycles of antiquity, and the first act ends with the chorus of the nations crying out of their suffering for a redeemer to appear.

As yet He is only dimly seen across an unfathomable future. His name is Emmanuel, who will visit and redeem His people. With this agonizing hope, the curtain falls on the Old Testament.

When it rises in the second act, there stands a young man in the midst of a Jewish synagogue. His name is Jesus. From His lips is re-echoed Isaiah's rhapsody of the Redeemer: "The Spirit of the Lord God is upon me; because the Lord hath anointed me to preach good tidings unto the meek; he hath sent me to bind up the brokenhearted, to proclaim liberty to the captives . . . to comfort all that mourn . . . to give unto them . . . the garment of praise for the spirit of heaviness . . ." (Isa. 61:1-3).

Then follows the remarkable proclamation of who this young man is. "This day is this scripture fulfilled in your ears" (Luke 4:21). Here at last stands the Saviour of mankind. "And the Word was made flesh, and dwelt among us, (and we beheld his glory, the glory as of the only begotten of the Father,) full of grace and truth" (John 1:14).

What does this vision mean to us today? At a time in history when mankind is threatened with annihilation, when all the hard-won Christian ideals are savagely attacked, when the pledged word of honest dealing is perverted by propaganda to cover a dagger which could easily slay what remains of righteousness, we need most desperately a vision of a new heaven and a new earth.

Never before has the Church been called upon to proclaim with such conviction that God reigns over the affairs of men. In the Bible is to be found the secret of justice among the nations. By sharing in the new way of life that it proclaims, each human being will find the inner peace he needs. Its divine message we must bring to those who know it not.

In 1917 Woodrow Wilson wrote this message to all American boys in the Army and Navy. It is still appropriate today:

> The Bible is the word of life. I beg that you will read it and find this out for yourselves . . . The more you read, the more it will become plain to you, what things are worthwhile and what are not . . . Whenever you read the Bible, you will know that it is the word of God, because you will have found it the key to your own heart, your own happiness, and your duty.*

24. The Meaning of Baptism

An Episcopalian knows that Baptism is the first Sacrament, but how many of us really understand what Baptism means?

---

* *Woodrow Wilson on the Bible*, American Bible Society, New York, 1928.

In the Episcopal Church most people are baptized when they are a few weeks old. Good church parents call their clergyman, arrange a convenient date, and choose sponsors. Until recently a baptism was a fairly private affair, held in an empty church when only the immediate family and their friends were able to attend. Before the eighteenth century most baptisms were publicly conducted during a regular worship service on Sunday. Frequently the main concern of both parents and their priest has been that the baby did not cry. Godparents are still chosen with little thought about whether they are practicing Christians, to say nothing of whether they are well-informed Episcopalians.

Sometimes parents neglect having a child baptized until by chance a priest calls upon them and persuades them to have it done. It is the experience of most clergy that parents rarely object. They usually are quite willing to arrange a baptism. In a vague sort of way it is obviously an important event which should take place. But there is the uncomfortable feeling that very few people could really say why!

It is a happy circumstance that this odd situation is changing widely throughout the Church. Many more Episcopalians today are far better educated in the meaning of their religion than they used to be. The clergy are requiring that parents receive specific instruction about baptism before it takes place. While the question of who is really qualified to act as a godparent is a touchy one still, it can be said that fewer are chosen today because they are merely friends of the parents.

Now let us think what baptism means. The most obvious fact is that it makes a child a member of the Christian Church. It is a public act in which parents declare their intention to raise the child as a Christian. It is an act by which the worshipping congregation publicly assumes responsibility for the child through the godparents. Both parents and the Church should be careful to select godparents who will really carry out their obligations. Sponsors are obligated to see that their godchildren receive a Christian education.

Yet baptism is more than a public ceremony. It is a sacrament.

This means that when a person is baptized, two things happen. There is an outward sign which occurs, and there is an inward change which takes place. Outwardly the child baptized is washed with water in the Name of God the Father, God the Son, and God the Holy Ghost. If baptism were only a ceremony of admission to membership in the Church, this outward sign would be enough. The Church believes, however, that an inward change takes place in the person baptized. Let us use for the moment the words of the Prayer Book to describe this inward change: when a person is baptized, "sin dies and a new birth unto righteousness" takes place.

It is obvious to any thoughtful person that man is a strange creation. Unlike an animal, he does not act according to instinct alone. He acts deliberately. This means that he can choose to act in one of three ways. He can act exclusively for his own benefit. He can act in the interest of a group of people. Or he can act so that it will benefit all people. If he benefits only himself, he is completely selfish. If he acts to help all men everywhere, he is a saint. Few people are thoroughly self-centered and few are saints. Consequently, the primary problem of living is to acquire the ability to act easily for the good of as many people as possible.

While we are not animals, we all are born with an inherited tendency to be selfish. This real fact about us the Church calls Original Sin. As long as we live, depending on how we have been treated by other people from the moment of birth, we shall struggle with the instinctive temptation to place our personal welfare ahead of the welfare of other people.

Now notice this important fact. We can only learn to feel and to act kindly to other people from long association with loving, kindly people.

When we are baptized, we are received into a fellowship of people whose principal purpose is to surround us with love, acceptance, and forgiveness. This fellowship is the Christian Church, which was founded by Jesus, the only sinless man in history. The relationship established by baptism with God's Son, and with people truly changed by their life in the Church, affects us deeply. We are influenced and shaped spiritually. This change in us, which starts to take place at the moment of our baptism, is what is meant by "death unto sin and a new birth unto righteousness."

While the theological words used to explain what happens in baptism are hard to grasp nowadays, the psychology of what happens in baptism is easy to understand.

Baptism creates a new relationship with God and with God's people, the Church. Nothing can ever change the fact that this new relationship has been established. That is why no one need ever be baptized more than once, and why, once baptized, no one can undo the effects of baptism. If anybody is not certain that he has been baptized, he may receive conditional baptism.

Obviously, baptism is the first step in the development of a Christian soul. Neither Christ nor His Church intended that baptism alone would automatically guarantee the salvation of a soul. Baptism was intended to be immediately followed by two important actions on the part of the Church. The first action is to expose the newly-baptized constantly to the Christlike influence of dedicated Christian people. The second action is to train the baptized in the household of Faith.

This raises serious questions. The growth of a Christian soul depends on the quality of the Christian life of many people. The first Christian exposure a baptized child will receive is from his immediate family. If his parents are warm and loving people, the child will feel the quality of their souls and will be influenced to respond in a warm and loving way to them. Yet it is only a short time before the child will require a larger fellowship to live in than his family. One of the first such larger relationships should be the parish church. Nowadays parents are encouraged to bring children to church as tiny infants, to expose them as early as possible to this larger family of Christ.

Consequently, a second serious question is raised. What is the quality of life of the congregation really like? Is it a gathering of individuals coldly impersonal toward each other, or is it a friendly and accepting fellowship? If the atmosphere of a parish is Christlike, this will communicate itself without a word being spoken. The degree to which it is really a group of loving people concerned

124

about extending, not merely courtesy, but Christian love to others is also the degree to which it will help the souls of children and adults to grow in Christ.

It is not easy for any congregation to achieve this highly developed Christian atmosphere. That is why there has been a phenomenal growth in family worship, followed by parish breakfasts, coffee hours, and classes of training for children and adults. The wide program which exists today to follow worship with opportunities for people to know each other, and to learn the Christian Faith, makes it easier for a congregation to create the necessary relationships which influence the growth of the soul. It is always intended that baptism lead to active participation in parish life. It is by sharing the relationships of a Christlike congregation that salvation slowly comes to him who has been baptized. As a child or an adult shares this life, he will be trained in the household of Faith.

Now to describe the true obligation of godparents in baptism. They do not represent a child's parents. Godparents are agents of God and His Church. Consequently, they should always be active, devoted members of the Church. If they are not, they are unable to take the solemn vows required of them as sponsors.

Listen to what a godparent must promise; these words of the Prayer Book are addressed to them:

> "Dost thou, therefore, in the name of this Child, renounce the devil and all his works, the vain pomp and glory of the world, with all covetous desires of the same, and the sinful desires of the flesh, so that thou wilt not follow, nor be led by them?"
>
> Answer: "I renounce them all; and, by God's help, will endeavour not to follow, nor be led by them."
>
> "Dost thou believe all the Articles of the Christian Faith, as contained in the Apostles' Creed?"
>
> Answer: "I do."
>
> (Prayer Book, p. 276)

These are only the first two of the six baptismal vows, but they are sufficient to make it clear that only a good person and a good church member can, with a clear conscience, give the required answers. When anyone is allowed to be a godparent who is not qualified, the relationship between a child and his church is damaged at the very beginning. The immediate effect of baptism on the child's soul is not stopped, but the long-range result of his Christian growth is reduced. All this implies that the clergy and parents should work more carefully together to obtain the best godparents possible.

Godparents do not assume any obligation alone. The whole congregation is responsible for the Christian growth of every baptized soul. Sponsors are chosen to make certain that a child is surrounded as early as possible by the whole life of the Church. They are expected to show exceptional concern for godchildren as long as they live. However, they have a special duty to see to it that their godchild is thoroughly instructed in the Faith and is presented to the bishop for confirmation.

Baptism is taught both by the Gospels and by the Church to be so important as to be called "necessary to salvation." We must strip away from Holy Baptism any crippling sentimentality which prevents it from doing what it is supposed to accomplish. Parents must be carefully instructed in the meaning of baptism. Godparents should be dedicated Episcopalians. Let us pray that God will fill every parish with His Holy Spirit so that every baptized person will grow in grace because he shares a fellowship which is truly Christian.

25. Episcopalians and Holy Communion

Episcopalians belong to a church with a long Catholic tradition. This means that our history did not begin with the Reformation in the sixteenth century. We, with other Anglican Churches,

126

Churches of Eastern Orthodoxy, and the Roman Catholic Church, share a way of Christian life that stretches back to Christ and the twelve apostles.

Nevertheless, the Anglican Churches cherish a freedom not permitted in the Eastern Churches nor in the Roman Church. We are not regulated by a central, infallible pope; nor even by a hierarchy of bishops and priests. The General Convention of the Episcopal Church has adopted, over the years, a Constitution and certain Canon Laws. The Constitution describes how the General Convention shall be organized, how bishops shall be elected, how new dioceses or missionary districts are created, what regulations are needful for the ordination of clergymen, and how the Book of Common Prayer shall be used. There are sixty-six Canon Laws which spell out in a more specific way a number of requirements covering a wide field, such as the consecration of bishops, Holy Matrimony, parish vestries, and theological education, to mention only a few.

The Bible and the Prayer Book describe what we believe, what our worship shall be, and what is expected of each member of the Church.

The Episcopal Church does not try to impose a totalitarian authority on its people. It carefully refrains from imposing external discipline. It sets high standards for its members. It rarely punishes those who fail to live up to them fully. It is convinced that the best discipline is that which is willingly accepted and conscientiously lived by the individual because he freely chooses to do so. It constantly hopes that those who are confirmed will look upon themselves "as free, [yet] not using [their] liberty for a cloak . . . but as the servants of God" (I Pet. 2:16).

With this in mind, it would be well to recall what standards the Episcopal Church sets for sharing the highest privilege the Church has to offer. The central act of our worship is the celebration of Holy Communion. To receive this sacrament regularly is our highest spiritual duty.

We find the regulations concerning Holy Communion in the Book of Common Prayer.

To begin with, who may come to the altar rail and receive communion? At the very end of the Service of Confirmation (on page 299), we find one of the laws of the Church concerning worship. It is called a "rubric." (It is so-called because in the early liturgical books of the ancient catholic church, these short laws were always written in red.) Perhaps you have never noticed this one. Yet it is very clear in its meaning. This is what it says: "And there shall none be admitted to the Holy Communion, until such time as he be confirmed, or be ready and desirous to be confirmed." In other words, the Episcopal Church does not permit open communion.

Sometimes the clergy of our church are asked why people who have not been confirmed cannot join us in Holy Communion. The answer is very simple. The Church has the right to offer its greatest sacrament only to those who have been sufficiently instructed and who have declared publicly before the bishop that they believe the Church's faith and intend to keep their vows made in baptism and confirmation.

Assuming that one has been confirmed, are any other things required of those who would make their communions? We find the answer to that question on page 293 in the part of the Prayer Book known as the Offices of Instruction. There it is written: "It is required of those who come to the Lord's Supper to examine themselves, whether they repent them truly of their former sins, with stedfast purpose to lead a new life; to have a lively faith in God's mercy through Christ, with a thankful remembrance of his death; and to be in charity with all men."

This rather long sentence says three important things. Before we make our communions, it is our duty: (1) to examine our conscience and repent our sin; (2) to have faith in Christ, with thanksgiving for His sacrifice; (3) to be in charity with all men.

We often forget these attitudes before we come to the altar rail; but the heavens will not ring with anger if we do, nor will we have committed any great sin. These are not laws. These are suggested standards. These are what Christians who enjoy freedom compel themselves to think about before receiving the indescribable mystery of Christ in the consecrated bread and wine of Holy Communion. These are three reasonable obligations. Who among us, unless he were sure he were clean and presentable, would think of going to dine with the President of the United States? By the same token, who is so insensitive that he would approach the Real Presence of God in Christ without giving thought to the cleanliness of his soul?

There is no one who is not strengthened by the faithful act of making his communion regularly. It has long been recognized, however, that it is easy for any well-intentioned churchman to grow careless in his personal preparation to receive Holy Communion.

How can we avoid this temptation? First, by training ourselves to say the General Confession in a way that applies personally to us. Do not be content just to repeat words. When we say that we "earnestly repent, And are heartily sorry for these our misdoings," think back over the past week. We will find some specific sin, the remembrance of which is truly grievous to us.

Second, by training ourselves to pay careful attention during the Prayer of Consecration, the Oblation and the Invocation. These are found on pages 80 and 81 of the Prayer Book. If we listen attentively to the words said by the celebrant at this deeply reverent part of the Holy Communion service, we will "[have] in remembrance [Christ's] blessed passion and precious death"—and we will join in rendering unto God "most hearty thanks for the innumerable benefits procured unto us by the same."

Third, we must take special care that we really are in a state of charity toward all people. If we are angry or jealous of anybody, we need to think twice before we come to the altar rail. We have no right to ask God to forgive us, if we are unwilling to forgive other people.

In the Episcopal Church no one will make us do these acts of spiritual preparation. If, however, we accept the personal responsibility to discipline ourselves, the rewards are very great. Men reach their highest achievement when they, of their own free will, strive to master themselves through God's grace.

26. Christian Belief About the Sacraments

Some years ago Stuart Chase wrote a book called *Words*. His object was to show how words live. When they are strong, lusty, full of life, they carry meaning! But sometimes words die! Their meanings grow cold. People no longer know exactly what such words mean.

Such a word is the word *Sacrament!* What is a Sacrament? What do we mean when we say, "the Sacraments of the Church?"

(1) First of all, it will help if we get one thing clear right at the start. When a person says, "I believe in sacraments," he means, "I have an explanation for the mysteries of this universe." The first thing to keep in mind is that *sacramentalism is a way of explaining life.*

Just as the word "democracy" is a set of beliefs about a government; just as "capitalism" is a set of beliefs about our economic system; so sacramentalism is a set of beliefs about life.

Sacramentalism is an answer to the question: "Is there anything behind what I see in the universe; and if there is, can I understand it?"

This first point must be very clear to us if we are to come to a larger idea of the meaning of sacramentalism. If one is not a sacramentalist (and there is only one opposite to the word "sacramental"), then one is a *materialist.*

A sacramentalist says, "Behind the material world, there is a deeper reality." The materialist says, "Nothing is behind it."

The sacramentalist says, "This material world helps me catch a glimpse of that other, deeper world." The materialist says, "You can't go any further. What you see is all there is."

That, therefore, is the first thing to remember about this whole question of sacraments. A sacramentalist is one who believes that the things of the material world around us indicate the real meaning that is behind them.

(2) Now that we see what sacramentalism is, let us put very simply what this means. What do we mean when we say, "The universe is sacramental"? It can be made clear by means of an illustration.

Take a dollar bill. What do we have? Well, to be absolutely realistic, all we have is an engraved piece of paper. To a man from Mars, it would represent nothing more than that.

But, to us, it is not just another piece of paper. To us, it represents a far deeper and more important meaning. That paper, to us, is an outward sign of a reality behind it. The reality is: one dollar's worth of value, backed up (we hope) by the United States Government.

That dollar bill is a sacrament. It is an outward and visible sign of another deeper reality. And the thing to see is, of course, that the important reality, the deeper meaning, is the invisible one—not the dollar bill, but the value which it represents.

Now the sacramentalist claims that all of life is just like that. Whatever we see in this universe, behind it is its real value, which gives it meaning. Behind a letter, with its outward signs of writing, stands the great reality: the message of a friend. Behind a wedding ring stands the reality which gives it meaning: the love of a faithful man for a constant woman. Behind a sunset is beauty. One sunset is only a glimpse of the great reality: Perfect Beauty. But it gives us some idea of what beauty is. Behind an act of compassion—a man stooping to pick up a tired child—stands the great value: mercy. Behind the death of Jesus Christ upon the Cross stands self-sacrifice: the reality of God's sacrificing love for each of us.

This, then, is the meaning of sacramentalism. A sacrament is an outward and visible sign of an inner and deeper reality. All of life is sacramental. The whole universe is a neat sacrament. Behind it is the invisible reality, an orderly intelligence, which we call God.

(3) The historic churches of Christendom are all sacramental

churches. This means that they believe that the best way to have quick access to God is by means of certain sacraments.

What, then, are the Sacraments of the Church? There are two great Sacraments: Baptism and Holy Communion. These were ordained and commanded by Christ.

There are also five lesser Sacraments: Confirmation, Holy Orders, Holy Matrimony, Penance, and Holy Unction—maybe you will remember them by the initials, COMPU.

Penance is the Sacrament which the Church provides for those whose consciences are heavy with the weight of *sin*. It is also called Sacramental Confession.

Holy Unction is the Sacrament of healing administered to those who are sick in body, and is found in the Prayer Book on page 320. It is not a Sacrament that is administered just before death, but is the ancient Sacrament of anointing and prayer for those who are ill.

These seven Sacraments: Holy Baptism, Holy Communion, Confirmation, Holy Orders, Holy Matrimony, Penance, and Holy Unction, are the means provided by the Church, in which, through outward symbols, a divine inner reality is given to those who receive them.

(4) Of all these Sacraments, the Holy Communion is the most central and the most important. The goal of the whole Christian life is only one thing: to become like Jesus was; for His character to be our character; His strength to be our strength; His outlook to be our outlook. When you become a Christian, that is your only aim— *to grow* to be like Him.

Now there are two ways to do it. One way is by long hours of self-discipline. We can acquire His character the hard way, by giving a large amount of our time to reading about Him, to thinking about Him. But most men cannot devote such long hours to such discipline.

Fortunately, Christ knew this and made it possible for us to become like Him, not by our striving alone, but by His help.

In the Holy Communion, the Church believes that His Real Presence is there. The Reality of Christ can be reached through the Bread and the Wine. Behind the consecrated Bread and Wine stands the most powerful personality in the universe. This Sacrament makes it possible for us to absorb—not achieve—the spiritual strength which was the secret of His character.

In this belief, modern psychology backs us up one hundred per cent. Powerful personalities impart their power to other people. In the Eucharist, the real, live personality of Christ comes into contact with our personality. If we approach Holy Communion properly, we receive His Godly strength. Through the outward signs of Bread and Wine, we come into the Reality of the Presence of God.

The Christian belief about the Sacraments is easy to understand. It is the belief that, behind the material things of the universe, there is to be found the Presence of the great Reality of God.

In Holy Communion, we have a rendezvous with Christ which gives us greater strength. Some unknown author has expressed it well in a paraphrase of the famous poem, "I Have a Rendezvous with Death," by Alan Seeger.

> I have a rendezvous with Life
> Within the Blessed Sacrament,
> When over me the priest is bent,
> And Jesus comes, exceeding fair;
> I have a rendezvous with Life,
> For He has promised to be there.
>
> I know I am not worthy thus
> To make His life mysterious,
> My sins are higher than a hill,
> His love is deeper than the sea,
> And so in my communion still
> I find His mercy healeth me;
> And I to my pledged word am true,
> I shall not fail that rendezvous!
> —Unknown.

V

OF MEN AND ANGELS

27. What About the Devil?

In contrast to other ages, there is very little preaching or teaching today about the devil. What has the Church taught about Satan?

To begin with, the word "devil" comes from the Greek word "diabolos," which meant the "accuser." The term "Satan," on the other hand, is older and derives from the Hebrew language. It meant the "adversary." Beelzebub is also a Hebrew word, which meant both the "lord of flies" and the "prince of devils."

There are only a few references to Satan in the Old Testament. He is the serpent who tempted Eve in the Garden of Eden. He is the evil spirit that provoked King Saul to envy David and try to murder him, as told in I Samuel 18:10. He is the evil spirit who tormented Job and caused all his misfortunes. In spite of these few references, there is no doubt that the people of the Old Testament believed deeply in the devil and evil spirits.

When you turn to the New Testament, you find many more references to Satan. It was he who tempted Christ at the start of His ministry. "Then was Jesus led up of the spirit into the wilderness to be tempted of the devil" (Matt. 4:1). After Christ had resisted the temptations, the Gospels record: "Then the devil leaveth him, and, behold, angels came and ministered unto him" (Matt. 4:11).

In the accounts of the healing miracles of Jesus, the Gospels often describe what took place as "the casting out of devils" (Matt. 9:34). And the Pharisees accused Jesus of healing by having the help of "Beelzebub, the prince of devils" (Matt. 12:24).

No doubt Jesus believed in the devil. In Luke 22:31-2 He said to Simon, "Behold, Satan hath desired to have you . . . But I have prayed for thee, that thy faith fail not: and when thou art converted, strengthen thy brethren." Even in so sophisticated a Gospel as that of St. John, Christ proclaims that "the prince of this world," meaning Satan, "is judged" (John 16:11). Finally, in the Gospel of St. Matthew, Jesus speaking of the last judgment, says that the souls of the damned will be cast "into everlasting fire, prepared for the devil and his angels" (Matt. 25:41).

There are numerous references to the devil in the Epistles of St. Paul and others. And all of us will recall the twelfth chapter of the Book of Revelations: "And there was war in heaven: Michael and his angels fought against the dragon [Satan] . . . And the great dragon was cast out, that old serpent, called the Devil, and Satan, which deceiveth the whole world: he was cast out into the earth, and his angels were cast out with him" (Rev. 12:7-9).

To this rebellion of the Archangel Lucifer and his casting out of heaven into the earth, the Church for many centuries attributed all of the troubles of mankind. It was believed that Satan would have power to tempt men until the last judgment. At that time Christ would come again in His glory. The devil, his fallen angels and evil people (living and dead) would be finally vanquished. After the final judgment, God would never be challenged again by Satan or by men. The Kingdom of Heaven would reign supreme in everlasting righteousness and peace.

If space permitted, we might trace what the post-New Testament Church believed. Such great theologians of the Patristic Period (A. D. 100-800) as Justin Martyr, Cyprian, Irenaeus, Clement of Alexandria, Origen, Athanasius, Basil, and Augustine wrote at great length about the devil. It is fair to say that Augustine presents us with the clearest statement. He blamed the fall of Lucifer on the sin of pride. Created like Michael, Raphael, and Gabriel, an archangel by God's loving will, Lucifer found it intolerable to obey God. He defied God and was, with those angels who followed him, cast out of heaven.

During the Middle Ages popular superstition about evil spirits clouded the clear, Biblically-based thinking of the Patristic Period. The farfetched, preposterous notions of that time were one of the causes of the Reformation. However, it is only fair to say that the

138

great theologians of the Middle Ages were never contaminated by the popular theology of thousands of poorly educated, superstitious priests and lay people. Two schools of thought developed in the Middle Ages about the devil among the great scholars. Great thinkers like Thomas Aquinas and Albertus Magnus taught that God created angels in a state of grace, but with free will. Like men, the angels were not given perfect beatitude. So, the fall of Lucifer came about, not because he wanted to be equal with God, but because he wanted to achieve beatitude by his own power. This became the prevailing idea of the Dominican Orders and remains so today.

On the other hand, John Duns Scotus taught that Lucifer wanted to be equal with God, and fell because of his immoderate love of his own excellence. This is the view of the Franciscan Orders.

The Reformation did not destroy belief in the devil either in the papal church, the Protestant denominations, or the Anglican Communion. All held the Bible belief that the devil is real. The papal church followed either Aquinas or Duns Scotus. Anglicans to this day, though they do not talk about it much, follow Duns Scotus. Most Protestants today, except the liberal theologians among them, believe in the devil, in his fall from grace, as the tempter of man, and as the ruler of hell. Generally speaking, among Protestant groups, the more fundamentalistic they are, the more frequent is their preaching about the devil and hell.

This brings us at last to the question: what does the Episcopal Church believe? It teaches that there is an evident power of evil at work in this world. We see it clearly in the sinful nature of each one of us, in the sophisticated conflicts of organized society, and in the savage struggle between the nations of the earth. Evil is a reality. No intelligent man would deny this.

The Episcopal Church teaches that Jesus believed in the existence of Satan. He identified Satan with the power of evil which we all recognize as real. The New Testament clearly believed in an order of beings known as angels and archangels. It was the Archangel Gabriel who appeared to Mary and announced the birth of

Jesus. It was a multitude of the heavenly host of angels who sang the Gloria in Excelsis on the night when Christ was born.

There are few Episcopalians who do not believe in the good angels of the Christmas story. Personally, if we can accept the New Testament teaching about good angels, I do not see why we should not accept the New Testament belief in a bad angel with equal ease. No other belief explains the existence of evil any better than the New Testament does.

So, if someone believes in a personal devil, there is no reason why he should not follow the thinking of the great theologians of the past two thousand years, and believe that Lucifer rebelled against God and was cast out of heaven. Satan personifies and causes all the evil that plagues mankind.

Since we have free will and will possess it eternally, we can choose here in this life and in Paradise to obey God or rebel against Him. Until the last judgment, the devil will tempt us. God will never force us to be righteous. If we eternally elect to rebel against Him, it is obvious that we will never be fit to dwell eternally with God in heaven. The human soul is eternal. It cannot be obliterated. Therefore, if it cannot go to heaven, it must go finally somewhere else. That place the Church calls hell, and in that place the devil and his fallen angels and the unredeemed souls of men will finally dwell. And, in hell, Satan reigns supreme.

This is the teaching of the Episcopal Church. It makes good sense.

28. Life After Death

There is a lot of superstition believed by members of the Church about what happens to our souls when we die. Some people think that as soon as we die, good people go to Heaven and bad people go to Hell. This is not the teaching of the Church. Such a belief is too comfortable, because nobody is good enough to go to Heaven at the moment death comes. Such a belief is also too cruel, because nobody is so evil when he dies that his soul will be condemned to Hell.

The Christian Church believes that the soul goes through three periods of existence. The first period is life on earth. This is called the Church Militant. It lasts from birth until death. When we die, our souls enter Paradise. This is called the Church Expectant. This period lasts from the death of our bodies until the Last Judgment. After the Final Judgment we receive back our resurrected bodies. In this third period we enter either Heaven or Hell. This is called the Church Triumphant.

Immediately after the body dies, the soul will remain completely alive. We will not become angels. Angels are Beings different from man. Each of us will enter Paradise as a human soul without a body. Nothing about us will have changed when we enter Paradise, except that we will not have physical bodies. Our souls will not be any better or any worse at first than they were at the moment of our death.

Some people develop beautiful souls while on earth. A beautiful soul is one that is honest, dependable, loving toward people, faithful to God, quick to forgive, self-sacrificing, kind, and charitable. Other people are selfish, hot-tempered, impatient, hateful, lazy, or self-indulgent. They grow ugly souls. Most of us are neither all good nor all bad. While we are alive on earth, our souls are a mixture of virtue and sin.

The first period of our existence, life on earth, is the most difficult one for the growing soul. There are two reasons for this. First, while here, our souls live in a physical body. From birth to death our bodies occupy a lot of our attention. They are wonderful possessions when they are young and healthy. But they sometimes become heavy burdens when they grow old or sick. Many of our temptations in life are caused by our bodies. We all want our bodies to look beautiful, to feel good, to experience pleasure. So God's great gift to us of a physical body easily leads us to pamper ourselves, to gratify bodily appetites, and to be vain.

Whether young or old, healthy or sick, our souls struggle to conquer our physical desires or bodily limitations. So in this life our bodies are both a blessing and a burden.

The second reason why life on earth is the most difficult is that here we are most separated from God. We learn about God from nature. We learn about God from mankind's long history. We learn about God from the Bible. We learn about God most because He became a man in Christ Jesus and lived for a short time on earth. We learn about God from the Church, which teaches us what Christ did and said. But we cannot see God, nor can we see Christ except through His Church.

Consequently, while we are in this first period of life, it seems to us that God is hard to know and understand. Unless we keep in touch with God daily, through prayer, Bible reading, and worship, His image grows dim in our minds. It becomes easy to forget how He wants us to live. The world about us becomes over-important. As a result, we find it easier to please ourselves than to obey God.

The temptations of the flesh and the fact that we do not see God face to face in this world make life hard for all of us.

But there comes for each person the time when his physical body dies. When death comes, we should not be overwhelmed with fear or sorrow. There is nothing to fear. Each soul enters Paradise. He will be welcomed there by Christ, and by loved ones who have gone before. And he will be welcomed by other faithfully departed souls. The only sorrow that should accompany death is the sorrow felt by those who remain behind that they are separated for the time being from someone they love. We should feel joy that the soul of our dear one is now in a life far greater than this present world.

What is Paradise like, and what do the souls in Paradise do? It is a place where the soul has opportunity to grow in beauty and goodness. But no soul is forced to do so. It is a place of higher development of our souls. It is not a place of ease. We shall have the chance to learn and improve our souls there. This will require effort from us. In Paradise we shall be given the chance to work to become a perfect person.

Paradise has two great advantages over life on earth. In Paradise we shall see Christ face to face. We shall not yet be ready to come into the Presence of God the Father. But the Risen Christ will be there often. Imagine what an inspiration it will be to know Him as the apostles knew Him after the first Easter Day! The power of His Holy Spirit will help us to desire to achieve perfection. Remember also that in Paradise we shall not be fighting against our bodily limitations. With the Presence of the Living Christ, and unhindered by the needs and desires of our earthly bodies, we shall find it easier to be as God wants all of us to be.

But! Let us remember one thing. In Paradise we shall still be free souls. We will have choices to make. We can choose to grow toward perfection there, or we can defy God's will and choose to disobey Him. Achievement of perfection is not automatic or quick in Paradise. Our souls will be there a long time. They will be there until the Day of Judgment.

In God's good time, each soul will appear before Christ for His Last Judgment. It is then that the decision will be made whether we are worthy to enter the eternal bliss of Heaven, or whether we are fit only for Hell.

The Last Judgment need not frighten us. We shall be judged by Christ and we shall be judged fairly. He was once a man and He will forever bear the resurrected body of His manhood. He knows from His own experience, while on earth and in Paradise, what a hard thing it is to be a man. He also knows that it is possible to become perfect. The Last Judgment is not a time of forgiveness. God always forgives us. Either we are worthy or we are not. Either we are fit to be forever in God's presence or we, by our choices, have deliberately decided to separate ourselves eternally from God. The decision is ours, not God's. God condemns no soul. We condemn ourselves.

What is Heaven, and what is Hell? Heaven is the joy of being at last in the Presence of our Father, God. It is eternal bliss, where the struggle to be perfect no longer is required, because perfection has already been achieved. It is the absence of all tension and the place of perfect love. It is to know God as He really is and to be known of Him. It is too wonderful to be capable of description by any words of man.

Nor is Hell a place of fire and brimstone. It is utter separation from God, from love, and from goodness of any kind. It is the most dreadful of all conditions, because it is eternal loneliness. It is the final separation of the soul from all creation. It is the state of perfect sin, which is the deliberate breaking of all relationships with God and other human souls.

At the Last Judgment we shall receive our bodies once again. At that time they will be like the body Christ had when He rose from the dead on Easter Day. They will be perfected bodies.

The Saints have passed through Paradise and are now in the Presence of God in Heaven. Today we give thanks for the example of their noble lives. Let us pray for the souls of all those who have departed this life. Remember that they are praying for us too.

Let us try to live each day in ways that will help us grow to be Christlike people. Let us ask God to give us the grace to kneel at last before His throne.

29. The Good Shepherd—Law and Love

There is probably no more beloved figure of our Lord than the portrayal of Him as the Good Shepherd. One thinks of tenderness, of kindness, and of infinite compassion, all of which was our Lord Jesus, and which vividly portrays what God is like.

But the teaching of the Church about Christ is something more subtle than just the simple figure of the Good Shepherd. In order to understand what else the Church is saying, look at the First Epistle of St. Peter, the second chapter; it says, "Christ . . . committed himself to him that judgeth righteously . . ." It talks about a judge.

So we have the portrayal of God as the judge, and the portrayal of God as the good shepherd. When you think of a judge, the first thing you think of is the Law. When you think of a shepherd, you think of Compassionate Love. These two things have to go hand in hand in the midst of our religion. This is an important lesson that the Church is trying to teach us. It has a great deal of bearing upon the life of each one of us and upon everything that is happening in the world today. We must have two things before us constantly: one is Law and the other is Love.

The danger in religion and the danger in life is that we try to take one without the other. When you have only law in religion, you get Phariseeism. You remember how misguided the Pharisees were in our Lord's day. They had very little in the way of love. It has happened to religion at other times in the history of mankind. This really is what happened to Puritanism. It became a whole set of legalisms, and man's real needs were forgotten.

On the other hand, if you have a religious outlook that does not make any room for law, which is the religious outlook of a great many Americans, then there is no personal discipline in religion. That is bad enough, but far worse than that, there is no thirst for righteousness, no desire to see justice done upon men. Such a religion is nothing more than a mushy sentimentalism. So we have to have in our religion a place for what the theologians call Law and Grace. They go hand in hand in real Christianity.

How did these two elements come into our religion? Law has been at least dimly perceived ever since man has been upon the face of the earth. Early tribal customs made up the first law. In Africa there are still tribes living in early primitive culture, and even these peoples understand something about law. There were great codes of law long before anything that we call modern civilization.

But the kind of law that has really meant something in historic times, and is meaning a great deal in the world today, is the moral law that gradually evolved among the Hebrew people. It all started with a man named Abraham. He was the chief of a little nomadic family, one of the many tribesmen going from oasis to oasis in the great Mesopotamian basin. He came to have one idea above everything else: that there was one God in the universe and that that one God required of him holy obedience. The Bible unfolds the story of the beginning of this in the Covenant that Abraham made with God. The Covenant was a legal contract. On God's part, He would take care of Abraham and his children forever; He would provide for them a special destiny among the nations of the earth. On Abraham's part, he was to believe in Jehovah; he was to obey what he knew of His law; and he was never to leave the land that Jehovah had given him.

Several generations went by and the descendants of Abraham did leave the land during a famine. Thus the Covenant was broken. They went down into Egypt and found it much more pleasant to live outside the Promised Land. Goshen was fertile; and they stayed on after the famine was over. Finally they were made slaves and were kept as slaves of the Egyptians for nearly four hundred years. Little by little, there began to grow up among the more sensitive Hebrews the idea that they were being punished by slavery because they had disobeyed the law of God. Law was beginning to take a tighter hold upon the minds of those people.

We know the rest of the story. Moses, a descendant of Abraham, who had been raised in the household of Pharaoh, came to feel the necessity to liberate his people. Finally he led them out of Egypt. What did he do when he took them away? He taught them the importance of the Hebrew law. There is not a religious Jew on earth today who does not look to the law of Moses as the leading guide of his life. When Israel finally did get back to its own country, there was one thing that had been burned into the Hebrew mind. This was that law was the most important thing in the world—the Holy Law of God as revealed by Moses.

The Israelites tried passionately to live according to that law and, with varied success, they did so for over a thousand years. Their nation became great. They dominated the world in which they lived. Then there began to be internal dissension. They split apart and they warred against each other, the north against the south. In the sixth century B. C. they were invaded by Babylonia and were taken away into slavery a second time.

146

During those years of harsh suffering, a new generation of men rose to interpret the Hebrew law in a new way. Among them were Amos, Hosea, Isaiah, Jeremiah, and Micah—the great prophets in the late Old Testament period. They saw that it was no longer just a question of keeping a set of holy rules. The law of God began to be interpreted in terms of a passionate thirst for righteousness among men.

Finally, Jesus was born. He went far beyond both the Law and the Prophets. Although our Lord said, "Think not that I am come to destroy the law" (Matt. 5:17), His conflict was with the people who were legalists, who had lost the vision that Amos and the other prophets had. Remember what Jesus said:

> Ye have heard that it hath been said, An eye for an eye, and a tooth for a tooth: But I say unto you, That ye resist not evil: but whosoever shall smite thee on thy right cheek, turn to him the other also . . . Ye have heard that it hath been said, Thou shalt love thy neighbour, and hate thine enemy. But I say unto you, Love your enemies, bless them that curse you, do good to them that hate you, and pray for them which despitefully use you, and persecute you; That ye may be the children of your Father which is in heaven . . .
>
> (Matt. 5:38-45)

See what a tremendous development had taken place in the two thousand years that led from Abraham to Jesus! From a simple understanding of a contract between a family and God had grown a whole nation's understanding of law. Then there welled up in the midst of the best of the Jewish thinkers a change that interpreted this law in terms of the desire for justice among men: ". . . what doth the Lord require of thee, but to do justly, and to love mercy, and to walk humbly with thy God?" (Micah 6:8).

Finally the greatest development of all came, when our Lord added to it the dimension of Compassionate Love. He taught His followers to sacrifice everything for other people in forgiving love.

Now, what has all of this to do with us?

Some people have blamed the tensions of modern life upon the discoveries of our age, particularly upon the atom, and they have

147

called it the Nuclear Age. They have said that it is because of this that men are so frightened and filled with anxiety today. Atomic power has a very great role to play, but the great publicity given to its dangers does not give the true picture of what is going on in the world.

This is the most passionate age of fierce idealism in terms of law and justice that the world has ever seen. That is the cause of this age of upheaval, and the atom is a side issue. Never before in the history of mankind have there been so many people who have been struggling for justice and a better way of life for every man. This is the thing that underlies the great struggle between the free nations and Communism. We believe that men will be better off if they are free and have individual dignity. Communism believes that ordinary people are too stupid and greedy to create a good society in freedom.

In our own country there is going on a very fierce and difficult struggle that is symbolized by public school integration. This is the question of whether or not every citizen of this country is equal before the law.

This struggle to find freedom and dignity is good. But we Christians must always remember one thing. We want not merely law. We want to establish a relationship of love between men.

This goal lays an obligation upon all of us who are Christians. Christians believe in law. But they also believe that to be true to the teachings of Jesus Christ, there is something that must be added to the thirst for righteousness, because the thirst for righteousness can make men hate each other. The thing that needs to be added to the struggle for justice is an overwhelming, compassionate love that forgives as it struggles.

In the early days of the Church, many Christians were persecuted and killed. Undoubtedly they were filled with fear, but they had two qualities that are unique in the world. Their fear was overcome by courageous faith. The Roman could understand courage because he was a courageous man himself. The thing that he could not understand, and this is what the world today cannot understand, was that as the early Christian was being killed, he prayed for the

148

Roman who was killing him. He prayed for the forgiveness of his persecutor.

So, if we are going to be real Chritsians today, we can't just be legalists. There is much more to our religion than thirst for righteousness. Nor can we be vague sentimentalists. That is not Christianity any more than Phariseeism is. Two things have to go together. There has to be a passionate thirst for righteousness. We have to enter into it; we cannot sit on the sidelines; we cannot have our heads hidden in the sands of the troubles of the world. The Church must take a stand. But at the same time the Church cannot take the kind of a stand that is taken by a nation; and a Christian cannot take the kind of a stand that is taken by a court of law. There has to be, in the midst of our great desire for the betterment of mankind, an overwhelming forgiveness and love for the rest of the world.

It is this kind of thing that we see in Jesus, who died for a better world. Upon the Cross He said, "Father, forgive them; for they know not what they do." The whole of the Crucifixion is Love going beyond the Law. When Love goes beyond the Law, then you not only get progress, but you also get reconciliation. That is the only way for peace among men. And that is the message of the Christian Church.

30. The Forgiveness of Sin

In order to understand what the Church believes about the forgiveness of sin, look at the following incident in our Lord's ministry:

> And, behold, they brought to him a man sick of the palsy, lying on a bed: and Jesus seeing their faith said unto the sick of the palsy; Son, be of good cheer; thy sins be forgiven thee. And, behold, certain of the scribes said within themselves, This

man blasphemeth. And Jesus knowing their thoughts said, Wherefore think ye evil in your hearts? For whether is easier, to say, Thy sins be forgiven thee; or to say, Arise, and walk? But that ye may know that the Son of man hath power on earth to forgive sins, (then saith he to the sick of the palsy,) Arise, take up thy bed, and go unto thine house. And he arose, and departed to his house. But when the multitudes saw it, they marvelled, and glorified God, which had given such power unto men. And as Jesus passed forth from thence, he saw a man, named Matthew, sitting at the receipt of custom: and he saith unto him, Follow me. And he arose, and followed him.

(Matt. 9:2-9)

Notice the element of faith present in the first half of this scene. It is central in the word "they"—"they brought a sick man"—and Jesus "seeing their faith." We do not know who "they" were. We do not know the sick man's name. It does not matter. They had evident faith. That was enough for Christ.

The implication of this incident in Jesus' life should bring hope and cheer to all of us. It says quite plainly that faith brings God's greatest spiritual gifts to us. In fact, it goes further than that. This incident proclaims that even if our own faith is weak, God can help us if someone else has faith.

How often we feel as if we carried the whole weight of the world on our own shoulders! I suppose there are many moments when the President is nearly crushed in spirit by the responsibility which lies on him. Such moments come to little-known people too. Each of us has undoubtedly said to himself at some time or other, "I do not know what will happen unless I solve this problem."

To all heavily burdened people the Church says, "Be of good cheer. You are surrounded by people who believe in you. Your limitations, failures, and shortcomings are forgiven. True, your faith may not seem very great to you. Yet it is greater than you think. God has faith in you. Your family has faith in you. Friends have faith in you. Even if you have no family or friends, the Church has faith in you. All of this means that you never have to make a

150

go of it alone. The key to life is faith. It is the only human condition necessary to bring a response from God."

Notice also in the Gospel story what Christ said first to the sick man: "Son, be of good cheer; thy sins be forgiven thee." Perhaps we wonder why our Lord did not immediately cure his palsy. Jesus understood people. Physical health is intimately connected with health of the spirit. A healthy soul is filled with vast contentment with everyday life. Quiet confidence under all conditions is its outward sign. Alas, few people have it all the time.

Instead, almost everyone is deeply aware of his shortcomings and failures. This produces guilt and anxiety. When we are worried, this is what is usually happening to us. Some guilt is normal in everybody's life. But excessive guilt is not natural. Far more than most people realize, they need to feel that they are really forgiven of their sins.

Christ knew that this was the case with the man sick of the palsy. If he could know that he was truly forgiven, he would be cured. God knows that this is true of human nature. So one of the most important works of the Christian Church is to proclaim forgiveness of sin.

Notice finally the adverse reaction of the Jewish scribes. They said within themselves, "This man blasphemeth." To the ancient Jew the authority to forgive sin belonged to God alone. Moreover, God's forgiveness could only be achieved by ritual acts of sorrow and by the offering of costly sacrifice in the Temple.

It is well for us to remember that Christianity differs from all other religions by offering forgiveness of sin quickly and freely. In the Hindu and Buddhist religions there is no forgiveness at all. Escape from existence is offered by a long series of reincarnations. All other great religions require expensive or difficult expiations for sin. This is not the Christian way.

We understand God as a loving Father. We believe that He loved mankind so much that He came down into human life in Christ. We believe that God in Christ possessed the full authority of the Father to forgive sin. We see in the Gospels numerous occasions when He told people that their sins were forgiven. We believe that Jesus delegated the power to forgive sin to His Church. We remember His words, ". . . as my Father hath sent me, even so send I you . . . Whose soever sins ye remit, they are remitted unto them . . ." (John 20:21-23).

Consequently, the task of the Church is to free people quickly and frequently from the crippling effects of sin's guilt. This it does in many ways. It teaches that God is a God of love, and not a God of wrath. It reassures us when we worship. Morning Prayer—Evening Prayer—each has a Declaration of Absolution, or Remission of Sin. In the Holy Communion Service the celebrant says to the congregation: ". . . Have mercy upon you; pardon and deliver you from all your sins . . ." The Church encourages the habit of private confession at regular intervals throughout the year.

It could be said in truth that the central purpose for which the Church exists is to provide a forgiving community in which the people of God can find the acceptance and security for which every person longs.

Christ spoke to the skeptical scribes: "That ye may know that the Son of man hath power . . . to forgive sins, (then saith he to the sick of the palsy,) Arise, take up thy bed, and go unto thine house" (Matt. 9:6).

Such a miracle did not just happen once. We in the Church see it happen all the time. Whenever our fellowship of love gives any person greater confidence, the same miracle occurs again. Discouraged people find hope. Anxious people receive courage. Young people grow into responsible citizens. Lonely people find friendship. Tempted people acquire strength. People without faith begin to trust. All these things happen daily in the Church. When they happen, they are the outward sign that sin has really been forgiven. This is what the Church is for.

VI
THE CHRISTIAN LIFE

31. How to Pray for Yourself

Should a man pray for himself? And, if so, how? Some people never pray much for anything else. Such people pray only when they are caught in a jam. Usually they do not pray often enough to know much about prayer. The result is that, when they pray, they pray in the wrong way.

In addition, there are some Christians who know so much about prayer that they have concluded that to pray for yourself at all is unchristian. They are right when they insist that prayer must be God-centered, not self-centered. But they are wrong when they assume that this literally means that we cannot pray for our real needs because this would be selfishness.

We need to go no further than to Christ to find our answer. He prayed often for Himself. If it was right for Him, it is also right for us.

If His example were not enough, we also have His plainest teaching. He expressly taught us the very way to pray for ourselves. He gave this teaching in a direct answer to His disciples after they had watched Him pray: "And it came to pass, that, as he was praying in a certain place, when he ceased, one of his disciples said unto him, Lord, teach us to pray . . ." (Luke 11:1).

It was in answer to this request that Jesus spoke the simple words of the world's most loved and best know prayer, "The Lord's Prayer":

> Our Father, who art in heaven, Hallowed be thy Name. Thy kingdom come. Thy will be done, On earth as it is in heaven. Give us this day our daily bread. And forgive us our trespasses, As we forgive those who trespass against us. And Lead us not into temptation. But deliver us from evil. Amen.

There are only fifty-five words in this short prayer. It is a master-piece of brevity. Twenty of these words directly show us how to pray for ourselves. Let us see what these words are and what they mean.

The first phrase is: *Hallowed be thy Name.* The beginning of all praying is adoration of God. This is true whether we are praying for the needs of others or for our own requirements. Christ put this right at the beginning of The Lord's Prayer. He did it for at least two reasons. First, it is the only polite and well-mannered way to talk to God.

Suppose a teen-age neighbor of yours were to ring your doorbell. What would you think if at the moment you opened the door, without bothering so much as to greet you, he said, "I need ten dollars. Please give it to me." The shock would certainly startle you. Such a request requires certain preliminaries. It would have been better if our brash young friend had begun, "Mr. Jones, I am sorry to intrude on you like this. You are such a good friend of my family that I was sure I could come to you. Father and Mother are not home and a situation has come up. I know they would approve of my coming to you. May I tell you what it is all about?"

This common politeness is part of what adoration in praying means. Just as no child who is well brought up should confront his elders with a demand first, so much the more should no mere human being breeze into the presence of Almighty God and start asking for things.

Yet adoration is deeper than mere politeness. It is the action of prayer which expresses to God our own unworthiness, no matter how great our need, over against His holiness, majesty, and perfect goodness. It is the only decent way a creature can come before his Creator. It puts our true relationship with God in the right perspective. When we greet God, we first express this relationship with language suitable to our respective stations. Adoration starts prayer out as God-centered prayer. We can adore God in very simple thoughts. Adoration is only some fitting way of telling God how wonderful we think He is, how much we appreciate Him and all that He is constantly doing for us.

It need take only a moment of our praying time. Jesus expressed it in a single phrase, "Hallowed be thy Name." Yet it is an indispensable moment which should never be neglected when we pray.

The second phrase is: *Thy will be done.*

Again, Christ is our example. Not only did He put this in The Lord's Prayer, but His own praying constantly reveals how He sought to understand His Father's will. Sometimes He could see what was wanted very clearly. Yet, there were other occasions when that for which He prayed found no easy answer. The most striking example of this took place in the Garden of Gethsemane. Jesus knew that if taken prisoner, He would surely die upon a cross. Like any other human being, He shrank from the physical and mental torture of a slow and painful death. He did not want to suffer and to die. As He prayed for guidance and for strength, the horror of being crucified became so startlingly real that the agony of His praying is more terrifying than anything that happened when He finally hanged upon the Cross. His own will cried out in all its weak humanity to be allowed to escape the Crucifixion. So great was His fear of what lay before Him, He prayed, "Father, if thou be willing, remove this cup from me . . ." (Luke 22:42). Christ was praying out of dire extremity for Himself, just as you and I must sometimes pray for ourselves. Yet He ended His prayer with words which decided the issue and drove the nails into His hands and feet: "nevertheless not my will, but thine, be done."

It is good that this scene is in the Gospels. It means that the purpose of a Christian life is to seek God's will and to do it. It demonstrates that when we pray, no matter how we want the issue to come out, the primary purpose of praying is to find God's will and get the strength to face it. So whenever we pray, whether it be for others or for ourselves, we must include some intention that God's will be done, and that His will, hard though it may be, become our will also.

The third phrase changes the emphasis from God and begins a series of three requests which deal directly with our needs. It is: *Give us . . . daily bread.* In this petition, we ask God to give us whatever simple things are necessary for our physical well-being.

There are four things which we need and which we cannot live without. We do not need them in such superabundance that we need to pray to God to have them except in moderation. We need food. We need a few possessions, like clothing, a home and furniture. We need some close circle of relationships with other people, like a family, or a group of friends. And we need good health. When Christ taught His disciples to pray "for daily bread," it was for these four essentials that He wanted them to pray.

Because we live in a country where most people can earn sufficient to provide themselves with food and more than a minimum of personal possessions, it would seem more fitting for us to thank God for the blessings He has provided than to ask Him to provide more. It is never right, when praying for ourselves, to ask God to give us great material riches and possessions. We can only pray for the necessities of life.

Yet food and shelter alone will not make a satisfactory life. Two other things are required for our physical welfare. One is a group of people to love and be loved by. The other is good health. Neither of these can be had as easily as food and possessions. Even when we enjoy them, they are so vulnerable that they can easily be swept away and lost. Therefore, much more time should be given in our praying to these two needs. The effect of praying that we shall have somebody to love and be loved by has an immediate good result in us. It makes us keenly aware that we have a large responsibility to certain other people. It makes us want to be more worthy of their love. We also quickly realize that even when we pray for ourselves, we cannot help praying for other people as well. Our own welfare is inextricably bound up with the welfare of someone else. We become less self-centered. We become for our very own sakes more gracious, more loving, more thoughtful, and more kind.

It is always right to ask God to give you perfect health. This is so, even when there seems to be no earthly likelihood that you can be made well again. This is one prayer for our own need when there should be no holding back in the extent of our asking. When it comes to health, we do not pray big enough. Miracles do happen in the most unlikely situations. Sick people do get well.

The reason why we dare to ask so much from God in the gift of perfect health is that we need health above everything else to do our work, to take care of the people who are dependent upon us, and finally to keep from being a burden upon those whom we love. For the sake of others, as well as for ourselves, we need good health. Consequently, much praying for our own needs should center upon our petition to be allowed to continue free from illness or to be made well again.

We are now done with praying for our physical necessities. Our last two petitions are requests for God's help with our inner spiritual condition. While they are two separate petitions, they go together so naturally that to pray for one and leave out the other will not satisfy us, nor will it do our souls much good.

There are two things every man wants for his inner life. One is to have forgiven the mistakes and wrongs done in his past life. The other is to get the wisdom, inspiration, and strength to keep useless burdens from growing in his spirit in the future. Christ understood this, and that is why He taught His disciples to pray for two final things for themselves: *Forgive us our trespasses* and *Deliver us from evil.*

In John Bunyan's *Pilgrim's Progress*, there is an allegorical description of the moment in a human life when the blessed realization comes that God has forgiven all past sin. It describes what we really are seeking when we confess and are sincerely repentant of our sins:

> So I saw in my dream, That just as Christian came up with the Cross, his Burden loosed from off his shoulders, and fell from off his back, and began to tumble, and so continued to do, till it came to the mouth of the Sepulchre, where it fell in, and I saw it no more.
>
> Then was Christian glad and lightsome, and said with a merry heart, He hath given me Rest by his Sorrow, and Life by his Death. Then he stood still a while to look and wonder; for it was very surprizing to him, that the sight of the Cross should thus ease him of his Burden . . . Then Christian gave three leaps for Joy, and went on singing . . .*

---

* *The Pilgrim's Progress*, John Bunyan, Rae D. Henkle Co., Inc., New York, pp. 35-6.

We want to drop the burden of the past. We know we can drop it because God has assured us of our forgiveness. Yet whenever we pray for ourselves, we need to take the time to go back over our day, face honestly our failures which have led to sin, and say sincerely to God that we are sorry.

Our praying for ourselves ends with a petition that we be delivered from any evil. Someone will doubtless say, "But haven't you left out one part of The Lord's Prayer? When we pray for ourselves, should we not pray: *lead us not into temptation* as well as *deliver us from evil?*" You are right; we should so pray. But they are both part of the same petition. Perhaps their connection can be more clearly seen if they are put together this way; lead us not into temptation except thou deliver us from evil.

God never led any man into temptation. It is the corruption of our own fallen human nature that causes us to be tempted, not God. Since we are human and weak, we shall be tempted not once but constantly in different ways through life. So was the Lord Christ. Even He could not escape temptation.

No, it is not to escape temptation that we pray. It is rather to escape the disastrous consequence of temptation. We pray that when we are tempted, we may be delivered from falling into the evil of sinning.

In this we need God's grace and we need it in abundance. We need the grace of wisdom to discern the right choices. We need the grace of inspiration to galvanize our wills to make the right choice when we know what the right course is. We need the grace of Ghostly strength to persevere.

These are the things for which a Christian prays when he prays for his own needs. If all of us pray like this, we may become the kind of men who are an honor to themselves and an inspiration to other men.

32. There Are Things You Have to Face

Everybody is familiar with the meaning of the word "escapism." When you seek diversion from the realities of daily life by going to a movie which transports you into a romantic world of make-believe, you are then practicing escapism. Mystery stories are said to be a form of escapism. Daydreaming is escapism. Excessive drinking is escapism. And what the word really means, of course, is that one attempts by these and many other methods to get away from real life.

Some of this escapism is quite good. Much of it is definitely bad. It is good when one seeks only temporary and beneficial diversion. It is bad when it is the result of a habitual attempt to run away from life.

There are things which nobody can escape. No matter how comfortable science ever will make our lives, certain things will have to be faced. No matter how paternalistic government may become, it cannot protect us from every contingency. There never will be a thoroughly secure and completely comfortable life. One grows up when one realizes this truth.

What are the things that everyone has to face?

First of all, you cannot escape yourself.

There was a newspaper story a few years ago about a woman in Chicago who had walked into a police station and said that she wanted to give herself up. Ten years earlier she had murdered her husband. She apparently had planned it well, and managed to escape detection. The police authorities pronounced her husband's death suicide. No one ever suspected her. She was quite free to come and go as she pleased. She had escaped punishment. The question of the nature of her husband's death never would have been raised by anyone again. To all intents and purposes, she had accomplished what she had set out to do and had escaped any consequences.

But there was one thing she could not escape, and that was the constant accusations of her own conscience. Every day it got a little worse. The terrible secret, which she carried for so long, grew and grew inside of her until it blotted out every other thought. And finally, in order to get relief from the accusations of her own mind, she had to confess to her crime. She escaped everything except herself.

One does not have to commit a serious crime like murder to experience this acute sense of discomfort which always attends in a decent person the knowledge of wrongdoing. Here is illustrated one of the simplest and most important rules of living: only do those things wherein you need never be ashamed, and only say those things for which you need never be sorry. If we will do this, we will be able to live quite comfortably with ourselves.

It is especially important, if we are to have peace with ourselves, to be thoroughly honest at all times. Do not promise more than you can fulfill. Do not pretend to be greater than you really are. Do not give other people the impression that many situations in your life are different than they really are. In the best sense of the word, "be yourself." You will be surprised to find how much of a burden is lifted from your life. Make the person you really are, and the person other people think you are, identical. If you do, you will get to like yourself in the right way very much indeed.

The second thing we cannot escape is hard work. Drudgery is not a desirable thing. It is no virtue to be condemned to perform a monotonous, little, tiresome, repetitive work over and over again until the end of our days. With the intelligence man has been endowed with, that kind of dreary work is sinful and unnecessary.

But nobody can become a very great person, or be a very happy person, who is not engaged most of the time in good hard work.

One of the most fortunate things for the human race is that most of it has to make a living. Unless there were the need to work, most of the great accomplishments of mankind would never have been achieved. On certain islands in the South Seas the natives are so abundantly supplied by nature with food, clothing, and shelter that they never have to work. But no great music, no great art, no great invention, no great philosophy, and no great religion has originated in the Islands of the South Seas. The need to work hard has produced the most accomplished men.

Even those who have wealth enough not to need to work for a living know that their lives will be extremely unhappy unless they are busy doing something useful. The need of the world is so great that there is always much good work for these people to do. But work they must, and work must everybody. There is no possibility of peace in life without it.

Happy is the man who loves his work. Fortunate is the woman who feels that what she does every day counts. Lucky is the young person who chooses a lifework because he wants to do that which he has chosen rather than because he thinks it is the best way to make money. The sooner one makes peace with the necessity for satisfying work, the sooner he will begin to get the maximum enjoyment out of life.

The third thing we cannot escape in life is suffering. Our ancestors, who lived before the days of our wonderful modern science, understood this better than we do. They knew that life could not be painless. They accepted it, developed a philosophy about it and, as a result, were able to take it when it came with better grace.

There has been a tendency in our generation for the individual to become disillusioned when suffering has come smashing into his life. We are prone to conclude either that there is no God, or that He is an extremely unjust one, if the comfortable tenor of our lives is seriously threatened. This is because we have forgotten that there is still a great element of risk in living. Every person, no matter who he is, rich or poor, intelligent or stupid, good or bad, as long as he is in this life is exposed to the same risks as everybody else. Sickness is one of those risks. Modern medicinal science has done miracles to help the suffering of sickness, but it has not eliminated sickness. The hospitals are still as crowded as ever. People still become infected with bacteria. People still develop terrible scourges like cancer and T. B. This is one of the normal risks of being alive. One should take the attitude that if sickness comes, it is no reason to lose faith in God.

Another risk is death. Everybody on earth knows that sooner or later he must die. He also knows that in the course of events all of his loved ones will die. It should not be a frightening matter, but it should be accepted as one of life's possibilities; and yet one of the most terrifying things to witness is the dreadful resentment against life and against God that comes to some people when one of their loved ones falls victim to this natural risk in daily living.

Now we should take the attitude toward these things that one takes when he plays an exciting and dangerous game. The rules are known beforehand. The risks are acknowledged at the start; the opportunities and chances of a reward are very great; but if in the course of the game we also get hurt, we ought not to ask to have the rules changed.

Nobody should go out deliberately to seek suffering. But it should not destroy one's happiness utterly when it comes, as it is bound to come to all of us.

Indeed, some of life's treasures have been learned and gained from suffering.

> I walked a mile with Pleasure;
>   She chattered all the way,
> But left me none the wiser
>   For all she had to say.
>
> I walked a mile with Sorrow
>   And ne'er a word said she;
> But, oh, the things I learned from her
>   When Sorrow walked with me!
>   Robert Browning Hamilton*

And the last thing nobody can escape is God. Some men find Him easily; others get to their belief in Him with great difficulty.

---

* *Masterpieces of Religious Verse*, ed. by James Dalton Morrison, Harper & Brothers, New York, 1948, p. 436.

There is no single way for all men. Yet, sooner or later, the question of God has to be settled for every man.

There is no question about the fact that the believer who has found his faith is better off than the one who has not. The religious man does a better job of living somehow. It is difficult to explain why this should be; but we know it is true. There is such a thing as the peace that comes with religious faith, and no life has really found itself until that peace is gained.

Francis Thompson understood this when he wrote:

> I fled Him, down the nights and down the days;
>   I fled Him, down the arches of the years;
> I fled Him, down the labyrinthine ways
>   Of my own mind; and in the midst of tears
> I hid from Him, and under running laughter.
>   Up vistaed hopes I sped;
>   And shot, precipitated,
> Adown Titanic glooms of chasmèd fears,
>   From those strong Feet that followed, followed after.
>   But with unhurrying chase,
>   And unperturbèd pace,
>   Deliberate speed, majestic instancy,
>   They beat—and a Voice beat
>   More instant than the Feet—
> 'All things betray thee, who betrayest Me.'**

A mind made up is a mind relieved. Facts faced are no longer terrifying facts. A mind reconciled to the inescapables of life is a mind ready to live a life to the full. Today, tomorrow, and every day you live, your spiritual strength will be required of you. That soul will be a strong one if it has looked without flinching at the things it has to face.

** *An Anthology of Famous English and American Poetry*, ed. by Wm. Rose Benét and Conrad Aiken, Random House, Inc., New York, 1945, p. 404.

33. Christian Forgiveness

Peter asked Jesus this question: "how oft shall my brother sin against me, and I forgive him?" Suspecting that Christ would not be satisfied with the earlier Hebrew teaching that "thou shalt give eye for eye, tooth for tooth" (Ex. 21:23-4), Peter suggested his own more generous answer: Shall I forgive after I have been sinned against "till seven times?" (Matt. 18:21).

He must have been flabbergasted by Jesus' reply: "I say not unto thee, Until seven times: but, Until seventy times seven" (Matt. 18:22).

This answer made crystal clear that there can be no limit to Christian forgiveness, but it leaves unanswered difficult moral questions. If this be required of us, how is it possible to uphold decent personal standards of conduct? Does Christ imply that we must shut our eyes to evil? Does He suggest that we leave justice undone? Can He mean that we should disregard the law of the State or the Church in order to make it easy for the wicked or rebellious person?

There is no easy answer to this dilemma. Obviously, no parent can allow a child to do anything he pleases. The United States cannot stand idle while Communism attempts to destroy the free world. Our large cities cannot allow teen-age gangs to terrorize their citizens. The Labor Movement cannot tolerate corrupt officials. A business executive cannot condone careless or dishonest employees. We cannot become spineless doormats when anyone tries to browbeat, injure, or exploit us.

Consequently, a Christian is always confronted with two demands. On the one hand, he must take a stand on the side of righteousness. On the other, he must never cease to be willing to forgive.

Christian forgiveness *begins* with our belief that God will forgive anyone who truly repents the wrong he has done. Because God's mercy is infinite, because He is ever ready to forgive, because we dare to hope that He will forgive us, we know that we have no alternative except to forgive those who injure us.

Jesus tried to make this clear with an example. In the Bible we read the parable of the unforgiving servant. He owed his lord ten thousand talents. It was a stupendous debt. Yet when he cried for mercy, "the lord of that servant was moved with compassion . . . and forgave him the debt" (Matt. 18:27). This very servant, however, immediately took someone who owed him a few pennies and had him jailed. When the lord heard about it, he was justly angered. His words cut like a whiplash: "O thou wicked servant, I forgave thee all that debt, because thou desiredst me: Shouldest not thou also have had compassion on thy fellowservant . . . as I had pity on thee?" (Matt. 18:32-3).

No one, therefore, has any right to expect God to forgive him if he does not show merciful forgiveness to other people.

If forgiveness begins in our theology, it becomes a *practical everyday* necessity in real life. A man or woman who will not forgive, slowly destroys himself and others. Most of the unhappiness in the world is caused by broken relationships with other people. Poverty does not cause unhappiness. Hard work does not cause unhappiness. Even physical illness does not necessarily cause unhappiness. That which does trouble people is relationships with other people that are broken in fancy or in fact. A broken relationship means that trust and love cease to exist.

Whenever a person is deprived of love, or feels that he is not respected, he will compensate for it in order to feel better. He may become mean and unbearable. He may even become vicious. More than likely, he will become self-righteous. Perhaps he will try to be superlatively efficient. The point is that in harshness, or in rigid orderliness, or in authoritativeness, or in the seeking of applause, there is usually an attempt to find a substitute for love.

This is so true that I venture to say that if you know anyone in serious trouble, back of that trouble lies at least one badly broken

167

relationship, and often a whole series of them. Remember, a broken relationship is a human situation in which somebody could not, or would not, accept and forgive another person.

If this is so, then the need to be able to forgive is not a pious theory. It is so important that it will make or break our lives. Because Jesus understood this, He taught that there can be no limit set to the need to forgive and be forgiven.

All of us live in a world of broken relationships. Consequently, we all suffer from the evil results of unforgiveness. Is there anything we can do about our condition?

The first thing is to be practical, and start trying to restore or improve our closest personal relationships. I would have some doubt about the effectiveness of any international peacemaker who cannot get along with his wife. A clergyman whose children fear him is unlikely to create an atmosphere of reconciliation among his parishioners. A business executive who is rude to subordinates will not for long satisfy his directors or his customers.

Therefore, the place to start practicing forgiving other people is in the home, at the office, and in daily face to face relationships. You and I cannot solve world problems, but we can be more loving toward our family and our colleagues.

Second, it is important to learn to forgive ourselves. Modern society educates people to be perfectionists. What heartache most girls endure because they will not forgive themselves for not being the prettiest person they know! Almost everyone projects an idealized image of what he wishes he were like. How many middle-aged men and women there are who find life so different from their youthful dreams. They will not forgive themselves. How much happier people would be if they could accept what they really are.

Is such forgiveness possible? Yes, it is. Only, however, if we have a real religion. The secret of self-forgiveness is a lively faith that God loves each one of us for no other reason than that we are His children. He loves us, not because we are beautiful, not because we are even good. God loves us simply because we are ourselves.

Some may say, "But how can I be sure that this is true?" Take a good hard look at Jesus, the Son of God. Do we find Him turning His back on the lowly, the disfigured, the sinner, or the poor? No! We find Jesus accepting all men on equal terms. As Christ found something lovable in all men, so God loves each one of us.

If we can forgive those whom we live with daily, and begin gradually to accept ourselves, we will find greater peace of mind. If each of us can create better relationships with those whom we see each day, perhaps we will help the world to find peace and a less anxious life for all.

34. Be Thankful for the Challenges of Today

The oldest marked grave in the cemetery at Plymouth, Massachusetts, is that of Governor William Bradford. The inscription on the monument reads: "What our fathers with so much difficulty secured, do not basely relinquish."

The United States, alone among the nations of the earth, has enjoyed unbelievable material prosperity in our lifetime. This is not to minimize the anxieties of the present day. Yet the fact remains that we are fortunate beyond all nations of the earth.

Consider the meaning of these words on Bradford's monument: "with so much difficulty secured."

Our high standard of living and our freedom were not easily obtained. They were made possible by the beliefs, privations, and sacrifices of hardy men and women who founded and developed America.

The first Thanksgiving Day was held in Plymouth Colony in New England. Why was it not held in England or Holland where the Pilgrims had lived for many years? The answer is clear. In the old country they had made sacrifices for their convictions. But they had not yet known hunger, famine, and death.

Doubtless they had frequently thanked God, just as you and I do when we say grace at meals. But gratitude became real for them when, after privation and suffering, they appreciated for the first time how lucky they had been to survive.

When the Pilgrims held the first American Thanksgiving celebration in 1622, they had learned by bitter personal experience what disaster was. During their first year as colonists, a large number starved to death. Whole families had perished from disease and hunger. Not one family was intact at the end of that year.

Finally, after heroic courage and hard work, they were rewarded with twenty-one acres of abundant harvest. There was not a sick person in the colony. The Indians were friendly. They were beginning to learn how to live in a wilderness. The future looked bright compared to what they had been through.

Their earlier thanksgivings had been a pedestrian, religious custom. This new Thanksgiving soared on the wings of the morning because it came from overflowing hearts.

Our beloved country has known many periods of hardship. The bleak years of the Revolutionary War brought our ancestors great affliction. They lost their homes, their businesses, and many lost their lives. Yet, after destruction, came rebuilding because there was the faith and courage to begin again.

We know what physical devastation the Civil War caused. Yet the Union was preserved and our forefathers, with vigor, turned to the stupendous task of settling and developing the West.

I do not need to remind you that our generation has fought two world wars and now lives under the constant danger of annihilation.

What has all this struggle been about? It has been to retain what our forefathers have with so much difficulty secured for us. It is now our privilege to maintain and extend to all of our citizens what others have won for us.

So we give thanks today, not only for American prosperity. We humbly give thanks for the struggles we and others have endured to free the spirit of man from the tyrannies of nature, politics, special privilege, ignorance, and the ambitious will to power by any individual or groups. So far we have pulled through. For this we thank God. What we have is not so much symbolized by shiny new automobiles, household comforts, or high employment. Behind these good, external things is the spirit of a free people, still able to give a good account of itself in the conflict and difficulties of our modern day.

Now let us turn to the other significant words on Governor Bradford's tomb: "What our fathers . . . secured . . ." What did they secure—and what must we beware lest we "basely relinquish"?

Our fathers secured the precious possession of freedom for each of us. All of us are acutely aware that our freedom and that of many other nations is threatened by Communism today. It threatens us by the possibility of war. It threatens us by scientific superiority in missile and outer space technology. This is potentially dangerous, and we desperately need to make every effort to recover lost ground. Yet at the moment, I believe this is not immediate.

If, however, Communism is increasingly able to convince neutral countries, our allies, and some of our own citizens that it is able to provide better homes, better clothes, more food, greater leisure, less racial friction, and a higher standard of living than our free system does, then we shall be really threatened! Russia and China are a long way from achieving this yet. But it is in these things that we shall be called upon to prove ourselves in the years ahead.

Communism will attempt to surpass us by strict discipline and ruthless disregard for human dignity. If we are to win this struggle, we shall need to demonstrate that free people are capable of self-discipline and great personal sacrifice for the welfare of people of all kinds.

Prejudice and selfishness are luxuries we Americans can no longer afford. Both are greater threats to our way of life than is Communism or war.

The freedom which our fathers secured for us with great difficulty can only be sustained by high convictions, hard work, a strong sense of moral values, and sacrifice. These are the very qualities which the men who celebrated the first American Thanksgiving possessed in such remarkable abundance. They lighted a torch in the darkness of their world. This light has sustained our nation through many crises and has made it strong.

Let us give thanks for material blessings. Let us give thanks for our families and our friends. But let us do something more. Let us especially give thanks that God has set our generation down in the center of a conflict which is so great that every human life on earth is now involved. Let us give thanks for the opportunity we face to write the most glorious chapter in the history of mankind. Let us re-consecrate ourselves to the same God from whom our fathers drew their inspiration and their strength. Let us dare to hope that we shall be worthy of the ideals and sacrifices of those who went before. Let us pray for an abundance of God's grace which alone can bring the peace and life we so ardently desire.

35. Four New Testament Commandments

On the last Sunday in Advent we look forward with joy to the celebration of the birth of the Christ Child. Yet the Prayer Book Gospels for the two Sundays which end the Advent Season are about John the Baptist.

This is proper because this John is famous in the New Testament as the spiritual leader who proclaimed that the Messiah was about to come. It was he who baptized Jesus and was the first to recognize Christ as the Son of God.

John the Baptist was born a few months before Jesus. He was the son of Zachariah, a Jewish priest, and of his wife, Elizabeth. She was a cousin of Mary, the mother of Jesus. You will recall that after the Blessed Virgin learned that she was to be the mother of Christ, it was to Elizabeth she went to confide her miraculous secret.

Eight days after the birth of John, Zachariah spoke the beautiful words of the Benedictus, so familiar to all who say the daily office of

172

Morning Prayer. It begins: "Blessed be the Lord God of Israel; for he hath visited and redeemed his people . . ."

Notice three of the last verses of this Jewish hymn; they not only foretell the supreme achievement of John the Baptist, but they also describe our task as Christian people:

> And thou, child, shalt be called the prophet of the Highest: for thou shalt go before the face of the Lord to prepare his ways; To give knowledge of salvation unto his people, by the remission of their sins . . . To give light to them that sit in darkness and in the shadow of death, to guide our feet into the way of peace.
> (Luke 1:76-9)

Nearly everybody has heard of the Ten Commandments of the Old Testament. Here in the Benedictus are found four commandments of the New Testament. Each commandment can be summarized in one word. The first command is "Go," the second is "Prepare," the third is "Give," and the fourth is "Guide." It will help us to prepare for Christmas if we remind ourselves what they mean.

To begin with, every Christian "shall *go* before the face of the Lord." You and I are the advance agents of God. Before the President of the United States makes any trip to other nations, members of the State Department and other agencies of our government fly to each city which he intends to visit. The President cannot go to Rome, Istanbul, Karachi, Delhi, or Paris, if his agents have not gone there before him and made various preparations.

God can only come to people after his ambassadors go to them first. God in Christ reaches people only through believing Christian people. From the first Whitsunday right down to the present moment, the first obligation of the Church has been to "go." The pagan empire of Rome was converted because the apostles obeyed Christ's command to "go into all the world." The Episcopal Church is here today because the Church of England asked missionaries of the Society for the Propagation of the Gospel to go to the American colonies. The church that "goes" is the church that "grows." It is an unfailing axiom of church life that where missionary zeal is strong, the spiritual power of that church is strong. If you want to kill a church, the easiest way to do it is never to mention missions.

The Christian duty to "go into all the world" must always be for the purpose of accomplishing definite objectives. Ecclesiastical locomotion is not an end in itself.

The Church goes to "prepare" a way for God. This is the second commandment in the Benedictus. How does a Christian prepare a way for God? He does it by supplying three things. First, a place to worship must be made available. Second, a program of Christian teaching must be started. And third, a real fellowship must be created in which individual people can be bound together into the family of God. This is true of any church, whether it be a simple chapel or a great cathedral. It is true of a city church or a rural mission. It is true of any church in the United States or of a distant missionary church across the seas. If a church offers only worship but does not teach its children and adults, it will be difficult for God to reach those who attend. If those who worship are all strangers to each other, they will lose much of the warmth of God's love.

Only when all three of these conditions prevail, is it possible to carry out the last two commandments of the Benedictus. Only then can the Church "give knowledge of salvation to his people" and "guide their feet into the way of peace."

Giving knowledge of salvation is quite a different thing from telling people about the facts of Christianity. Anyone can learn about the Christian religion. It is much more difficult to become truly religious. An intelligent adult can acquire many of the important facts of Christian thought in a few months. But this will not necessarily make him a believing, practicing Christian, who is truly aware of the saving grace of God at work in his own life. Without this awareness of salvation, no Christian can be guided into the way of peace of mind and heart.

Whether or not we realize it, each one of us seeks salvation and peace more than any other thing in life. Most people try to find it in ways that are not religious. This does not imply that all such ways are bad.

174

The organization man tries to find it by making a secure place for himself in a business which will provide increasing opportunity and a larger income. The beatnik tries to find it by rejecting the conformity of competitive modern life. Communists try to find it in a regimented social order. The alcoholic tries to find it by escape from reality. A street gang member seeks it by belonging to a group which gives him status. The growth of the welfare state is a world-wide indication of man's longing for earthly salvation and peace.

These and many other attempts to grasp hold of security all lack two essential things. Salvation and peace are the fruits of love and trust. Men love and trust each other better when they believe in God. They are able to love and trust each other best of all when they believe in the God whom Jesus Christ revealed.

It was John the Baptist who first recognized that Jesus was the Son of God. He it was who proclaimed that the Messiah was nigh at hand. Because John lived up to the prophecy uttered by his father, Zachariah, he leads us still to the celebration of Christmas Day.

36. A Lenten Rule

No conscientious churchman should hurry into Lent without giving thought. Shrove Tuesday is a poor day upon which to decide what your use of Lent will be. He who makes a few hasty Lenten resolutions on Ash Wednesday usually finds his high resolves dwindling before the following Sunday. Therefore, plan ahead if you would make Lent count for your spiritual growth.

How can we use Lent well? Listen to what Isaiah the prophet has to say:

> Sing, O barren, thou that didst not bear; break forth into singing, and cry aloud . . . Enlarge the place of thy tent, and let them

stretch forth the curtains of thine habitations: spare not, lengthen thy cords, and strengthen thy stakes.

(Isa. 54:1-2)

The important words in this portion of Holy Scripture are big, powerful verbs. They can be our clue to a Lent of spiritual growth.

The first word is *sing*. "Sing, O barren, thou that didst not bear."

The proper spirit with which to keep a Holy Lent is to have in our hearts the ordinary cheerfulness that always accompanies the prospect of a stimulating and worthwhile adventure. Lent is a special opportunity to become a better person. It is a short, intensive training period for the improvement of the body and the soul. It is a month and a half of jolly good fun wherein we engage in a real tussle with ourselves.

This is precisely what our Lord Jesus meant when He gave His famous rules for keeping a fast:

> Moreover when ye fast, be not, as the hypocrites, of a sad countenance . . . But thou, when thou fastest, anoint thine head, and wash thy face; That thou appear not unto men to fast, but unto thy Father which is in secret. . . .

(Matt. 6:16-18)

Cheerfulness is the spirit with which to enter Lent. Sing, and give thanksgiving to God for the opportunity it brings us to remember God's love for us in Christ. Sing, and give praise to God by voluntary abstinence and self-discipline. Sing, and no longer be barren of the good works of the Lord.

The second cue word is *enlarge*. "Enlarge the place of thy tent, and let them stretch forth the curtains of thine habitations."

The prophet is reminding the Jewish people of a scene that is familiar to every dweller in the desert country. He pictures for them the colorful oasis tent of the nomad. Because it had to be taken down and compactly folded for camel travel to the next water hole, the average tent never seemed to have quite enough room. I suppose times have not really changed. Just as the young couple in a small apartment long for just one additional room when their family begins to grow, so the Jewish desert wanderer always yearned to have a little larger tent. But a larger tent, like a larger apartment, is only likely to come to those who put forth the effort to earn one.

Now Isaiah was not really talking about tents. All of us inhabit narrower and more cluttered mental halls than we need to dwell in. "Enlarge the place of thy tent" is a valid Lenten call to each one of us to grow into a more spacious knowledge of our religion.

How large is our habitation of knowledge about our church? Do we know the common facts about the Bible, our church, our theological beliefs, our sacramental life? We can't simply be satisfied with what we now know. We must use Lent to "stretch forth the curtains of [our] habitations."

The third cue word is *lengthen*. "Lengthen thy cords."

If you have been a summer camper, you undoubtedly have been initiated into the mystery of the successful operation of a tent. You will recall that most tents are so made that cords of strong rope branch outward from the sloping roof to hold the top of the tent in place. These ropes are never knotted tight when they are secured. Instead, they are fitted with a movable loop so that they can quickly be lengthened or shortened as need arises. The length of a tent-cord depends upon the strain which weather puts upon the rope.

Isaiah has used a striking illustration here. He calls to us to "lengthen [our] cords." The ropes of a tent are always lengthened in stormy weather to ease the strain.

One of the most important uses of Lent is that it can be a time when we relieve the strain upon our daily lives. Nearly every one of us lives under a busy schedule of activities. We rush from one appointment to another, in frantic haste. Life today is high-speed life. We subject our tortured nervous systems to a kind of punishment they were never intended to endure. We rush through day after day, fall wearily into bed at night, and wake up exhausted in the morning. The result is that, for many, there is no real joy to living. Excitement there is a plenty, but "the peace of God which passeth understanding" is an empty Prayer Book phrase. How few there are who know what it means to have the gladness of thanksgiving in their hearts, or who face each morning with the attitude, "This is the day which the Lord hath made; we will rejoice and be glad in it."

This futile fury of modern living need not be! It is taking years off the life-span of many people. It kills more of our neighbors than any other dangerous thing.

Lent is a time to "throttle-down." For six weeks, we should reduce the breakneck speed at which we are going. This is one of the reasons why the Church wants us to "give up" things for Lent. No Lent is well kept unless we obey the call of our Master Jesus Christ, when He said to His disciples: "Come ye yourselves apart into a desert place, and rest awhile" (Mark 6:31).

Each of us alone will know best what to take out of our daily schedules. Maybe it will be the bad habit of staying up too late at night. Maybe the social calendar needs to be radically reduced. Maybe we are serving on too many committees. More people today are nervous from trying to be perfect than from the dissipation of being naughty! Or maybe we are time-wasters, who put off until the last minute the things we ought to do with orderly leisure, and then madly drive ourselves into a frenzy to do them all at the last moment. If so, Lent is the time to get some order into life.

Whatever our besetting sin—which causes us to live intensely— whether it be pride or sloth, we must face it honestly, and get rid of it during Lent.

"Enlarge thy cords." Relax the strain!

The last cue word is *strengthen*. "Strengthen thy stakes."

This is the call each one of us receives in Lent to drive deeper the shafts which secure our inner lives.

One thing in the Lenten observance is basic to all the rest: taking the time to pray! If we try to grow without praying, we will fail miserably.

Dr. Lewis L. Dunnington tells in a sermon what prayer means to Roland Hayes, the great Negro concert singer, who maintains that he never could have faced his burdens if he had not prayed constantly for help. When asked how he maintained his serenity, Hayes said that he tried to live every moment with such consciousness of the Divine Presence in his heart that every trace of bitter-

178

ness should disappear. He never began a concert without standing silent before his audience, praying for God's help.

Prayer makes many things possible. It makes one forgiving. It puts people and events in the right perspective. It strengthens our capacity to live well.

For a Lenten rule, there is none better than these four words from the first two verses of the fifty-fourth chapter of Isaiah: sing, enlarge, lengthen, and strengthen.

37. My Duty as a Churchman

One of the most tender scenes in the New Testament is that of the Adoration of the Magi. It tells the story of the visit of the Three Wise Men to the manger of the infant Jesus at Bethlehem. I want you to think about the Wise Men. They were people of different races. One was an Asiatic, one was a man with a brown skin, and one was a white man. This is what the Church should be: a fellowship of God's children bound together by a common faith in the Lord Jesus Christ and in true brotherhood toward each other.

Just as we are like the Wise Men in this respect, I hope we will be like them in three other ways.

Notice what they were doing with their eyes! The Magi were astrologers and ancient seers. Though they came from different countries and different races, they had one thing in common. They were well educated in the writings and prophecies of the ancient world. It had been prophesied that someday a great star would appear in the East. And when it came, it would proclaim the birth on earth of the Son of God, the King of Kings. So each of them scanned the heavens with his eyes, and finally they saw the Star, each from his distant land. What their eyes had seen, they followed until it led them to Christ.

Their eyes had recognized God's revelation and they followed.

The Second Office of Instruction in the Prayer Book says that our first duty as a member of the Church is to follow Christ. We must be like the Wise Men then, and keep our eyes open every day of our lives to follow our Lord and Master. To follow Christ it is necessary to know all that we can about Him. The best way to do this is to read our Bibles.

The Bible is the best-selling book in the world. Year after year, more copies of the Bible are published and distributed than any other book. There are many people in the world who would rather have a Bible than any other possession. It is a source of inspiration, faith, and courage for countless millions. In view of its central place in our religion, it is surprising how many Episcopalians know so little about the Bible.

Two suggestions may help to overcome this lack. Read a book which will help you understand the whole Bible quickly. Such a one is *The Holy Scriptures,* written by Dr. Robert C. Dentan of General Theological Seminary; it is one of a series of six books in the Church's Teaching Series, and you will find it very interesting. Then start a regular habit of reading your Bible daily. One of the best ways to do this is to follow the lectionary, or table of daily lessons, in the front of the Prayer Book. Have your Bible and Prayer Book at your bedside. Just before you go to sleep, read the verses suggested for each day. It will relax you. Slowly you will find the teaching of the Bible and the life of Christ soaking into your mind. Thus, by using your eyes, you will fulfill your first duty as a member of the Church. You will see Christ more clearly each day, and seeing, you will follow Him.

The Wise Men also did something with their hearts. After their paths had met, they decided to travel together. The star went before them until they arrived in Jerusalem. Remember, they were looking for a king. They were also very learned astrologers. They had served in the palaces of their own lands as trusted advisers to their local kings. What could be more natural than that they go first to King Herod's court in Jerusalem!

When he heard that there were ancient prophecies that proclaimed the coming of a king who would be the King of all kings,

Herod was filled with jealousy and fear. He summoned his own wise men and demanded to know where Christ should be born. Their answer terrified him because they said, "In Bethlehem of Judea: for thus it is written by the prophet . . . for out of [Bethlehem] shall come a Governor, that shall rule my people Israel" (Matt. 2:5-6).

Herod was a crafty politician. He knew full well that he had no real claim to the Hebrew throne. He had been made a king by the Roman conquerors. It was the policy of Rome to govern foreign provinces through the pretense of a local native king. The power behind the throne was the Roman procurator. So after Herod had recovered somewhat from his fright, he told the Wise Men to go to Bethlehem and find the infant King, and that when they had found Him to return to his court and let him know where the Baby was, so that he might go and worship Him also.

The Wise Men went to Bethlehem, where they found Jesus. Now notice what they did. They knelt before Christ and their hearts were filled with adoration! They worshipped Him. They poured out their love and homage. And loving Jesus, they decided not to return to Herod suspecting that he meant to kill Jesus. "They departed into their own country another way" (Matt. 2:12).

What does the Office of Instruction say is our second duty as a member of the Church? To do just what the Magi did. To worship God. They did it in a stable and they did it only once in their lives. We are much more fortunate than they. We are asked to do it every Sunday in a church.

The whole of life boils down to two choices. We can reject the claim of Christ's Kingship as Herod did. Or we can accept Him as the Wise Men did, and worship Him. The world has always been faced with a terrible alternative as far as Jesus is concerned. If he really is God, then we must go the whole way and pay Him the homage due God. If He isn't God, then He has to be killed. Herod was the first human being to face this test. He decided to kill, and you recall that when the Wise Men did not return, he ordered that all male children in his kingdom, under two years of age, be slain. This is called the Slaughter of the Holy Innocents. We remember that historic tragedy each year on Holy Innocents' Day, three days after Christmas.

This was the choice the Pharisees had to make during Christ's ministry. How often we are told that they took up stones to kill Him. This was the choice the high priests and the Sanhedrin had to make at Jesus' trial. They rejected Him as God and nailed Him to a cross. This is the choice the world has always had to make since then. When Jesus came into conflict with private ambition, personal greed, human pride, or national and racial aspiration, and the chips were really down, then men have chosen sides. Some have killed Him and some have worshipped, adored, and died in a thousand ways for Him.

Notice, finally, what the Magi did with their hands! They brought gifts and laid them before the infant Jesus. A human hand is one of the most expressive features of a person's body. A hand offered to another is a sign of welcome, acceptance, friendship. A hand hardened by honest work, or made supple by an artist's skill, is that person's chief tool. Hands clasped in supplication are an outward sign of inward prayer.

What does the Office of Instruction say is our third duty as a member of the Church? "To work, to pray and to give for the spread of God's kingdom." All of these three things are expressed by our hands! God does not have very much use for an empty or idle hand!

Now, please, don't think that we churchmen of the historic Episcopal Church are like the Puritans. It does not mean that we must be forever busy and never have any fun or relaxation. On the contrary, it is desperately important that we should find ways to throw off our personal and business problems.

> The world is too much with us; late and soon,
> Getting and spending, we lay waste our powers:
> Little we see in Nature that is ours.
>
> William Wordsworth*

* An Anthology of Famous English and American Poetry, ed. by Wm. Rose Benét and Conrad Aiken, Random House, Inc., New York, 1945, p. 207.

Yet, no one can escape responsibility. God needs you. Your family needs you. Your friends need you. Your work needs you. Your church needs you. You need you! All of this need has never been summed up better than by the three words: work, pray, give.

Notice that in the Office of Instruction these three words come last among our duties as a member of the Church. This does not mean that they are less important! It illustrates the psychological accuracy of the Christian religion. They are placed last because no man can work at anything well, nor pray effectively, nor give of himself or his possessions unless he first sees something worthwhile to follow and adores that which he sees. Belief and worship supply the spiritual power to work, prayer, and giving.

In an age conditioned by science, each one of us knows the importance of finding a formula that will unlock the secrets of the universe. Einstein's famous formula, $E = mc^2$, released the secret power of the atom. We also need a formula to live by. A man's spiritual being is subject to God's law just as the physical world is. A formula is not a beautiful picture which describes in detail the whole wonder of creation. It is a working basis for describing reality simply. It is a blueprint which points toward what can be accomplished.

There is no more simple formula for the good life than this: follow Christ; worship God; work, pray, and give. It will require the whole man: mind, heart, and bodily activity.

38. Bring Forth Fruit with Patience

The famous teaching of Jesus known as the Parable of the Sower describes the four ways people respond to God.

Jesus had a remarkable gift for saying the most profound truth in a simple illustration. In this parable He pictures a farmer sowing seed by hand. You see the farmer walking slowly through his field. As the seeds fall, they settle in four distinct places. Some fall on the edge of a roadway. Some land upon rocky ground. Some are scattered among bushes of thorn. And others fall on good, rich soil.

Apparently the people who heard Jesus tell this parable were slow to get its point. It is one of the few He ever explained. The seed, He said, is God's word! That part of it which fell on the heavily travelled road never amounted to anything. It was either trodden down by the passing events of the world, or was gobbled up by hungry birds! There was absolutely no response to God.

This seems to be so true of the world today. Little of daily life has any place in it for God! We rush about our occupations and rarely ask any question about what we are doing except, "are we making enough money?" or "is our work congenial?" or "are we as efficient as we would like to be?" It is a rare Christian who takes the trouble to ask, "Is what I do daily really pleasing to God?" His word is trodden down by busy self-absorption in what we like to call the "practical affairs of life." To such people God is shut out, or at best is an affair for Sunday morning.

Jesus was also saying something else at this point in the parable. God is not only ground underfoot by the petty events of life, but worse than that, we each are tempted to use God for our own selfish purposes! We take the word of God, which was meant to change us, and we exploit it to forward our ambitions. History is full of appalling atrocities committed under the excuse that they were the will of God. The politician who gets elected because he exploited the Catholic vote, the Jewish vote, or the Protestant vote is using God. The new super-patriot, who holds the Bible in one hand and the Constitution of the United States in the other, while he denounces civil rights for every American citizen different in race or creed from himself, is using God. The person who joins a church for the sake of social prestige is using God. This is seed which has fallen by the wayside. In the process God gets trampled underfoot. Jesus had little respect for anyone who used the cloak of religion to mask his attempts to protect his personal interests.

184

The second seed, said Christ, fell on thin and rocky soil. People like this receive the word of God with joy. Then when the first temptation comes, their religion withers and dies because it has no root. Every Christian Communion has on its membership rolls people just like that! There are many such in the Episcopal Church.

We make it too easy to become a communicant of the Episcopal Church. We confirm children when they are too young! We do not teach well enough or long enough! We ask no probationary period beyond a few short weeks, in which the sincerity of prospective members is truly tested! We rarely follow up the act of confirmation with personal consultation or confession! As far as the Episcopal Church is concerned, we cannot blame the shallow-rooted people, who quickly fall away. Instead, we should blame our easygoing methods of Christian training. In these days of threat to the very existence of Christianity, Anglicans, and our Protestant brothers, can no longer afford to present the Christian religion to people as one that requires no accepted disciplines. Our biggest single internal problem is the church member who has shallow roots and who quickly falls away.

Then Jesus described the third kind of Christian. He is the product of seed that fell among the thorns. These grow, develop roots, but become "choked with cares and riches and pleasures of this life, and bring no fruit to perfection" (Luke 8:14). We can have a deep feeling for these church members. Basically, in their hearts, they really desire God. Then, what life does to them chokes their religion out of them. Notice how Christ groups together an unusual collection of thorns: "cares, riches, and pleasures." He is saying that an excess of bad things and an excess of good things are likely to be equally damaging to our response to God.

How true this is of many people! There are church members whose religion cannot stand up under heavy personal burdens or increased prosperity. Burdens make it seem that God does not care! Wealth and pleasure make it seem as if God is not necessary! Cares frequently destroy belief. Good fortune too easily produces over-confidence in self. We should have the greatest compassion for these Christians! They are never entirely lost. They do have good

185

roots. Very frequently they can be reached. There surely is always hope for them. As church people, we should always be ready to reach out in love to help them find God again.

And, finally, Jesus spoke of the seed that fell on good ground. These are they, "which in an honest and good heart, having heard [God's] word, keep it, and bring forth fruit with patience" (Luke 8:15). These people are the backbone of the Church! They are to be found in every parish! They are in church every Sunday! They pray! They work! And they give generously for the spread of Christ's kingdom! They are the calm, reliable people, who in their hearts know the deepest satisfaction of a sturdy faith. They are the strong right hands of the clergy, who give thanks for them every day. They are a joy to God, because He knows that it is souls like theirs that make His agony upon the Cross worthwhile. If you want a short description of what a good Christian is, it is this: "He keeps the word of God, and brings forth fruit with patience."

39. About Man's Salvation

Jesus told a story called the Parable of the Wedding Feast to illustrate a truth. He told the story primarily to explain why He spent so much time with common ordinary people, who were considered both sinful and not very religious.

He described the kingdom of heaven as the situation in which a certain king made a marriage for his son. Invitations were sent out to all the better people. To the king's astonishment, the invited guests declined to come. Believing that they must have misunderstood him, the king sent his servants out a second time. An explanation accompanied the repeated invitation. Not only was the prince to be married, but the wedding feast was all prepared. This was to be a gala festival. This time the refusals were point-blank insults to the king's dignity. Some brushed off the invitation with shallow explanations that they were needed at the farm. Others made hasty excuses about the urgency of business matters. The rest did even worse. They slaughtered the king's servants. At that point, the king's astonishment turned into anger. 'If that is the way they feel,' said he to his other servants, 'they are not worth consideration. Go out in the streets and bring in the common people.'

Up to this point the meaning of the parable is crystal clear. God is the King. Repeatedly, for centuries, He had called the leaders of the Jewish nation to share His joy. Instead, small personal interests preoccupied them. God's servants, the prophets, had frequently been killed. Now, at last, Jesus was taking God's case to any Jew who would listen to Him.

If the parable had stopped there, we would have been perfectly in agreement. The king was right to snub the snobbish and the selfish elite. After all, heaven is open to everybody. It was true democracy when the ordinary fellow in the street was invited in. But the parable did not stop there. Jesus added a real shocker.

After the wedding had been furnished with guests, both bad and good, the king came in to look them over. One caught his attention. "And he saith unto him, Friend, how camest thou in hither not having a wedding garment? And he was speechless. Then said the king to the servants, Bind him hand and foot, and take him away, and cast him into outer darkness . . . For many are called, but few are chosen" (Matt. 22:12-14).

Our instant response is that of outraged justice. How fickle of the king, we feel, after opening the feast to everybody, to condemn a man simply because he did not happen to be wearing a wedding garment. On the surface it looks as if the king is even more superficial than those at whom he was originally angered for not coming to his party. At least they had some excuse. It just does not seem fair to throw out a man because he was not wearing the right clothes!

What is the explanation of Christ's story?

You will see that the episode of the missing wedding garment is neither a codicil to the first part of the parable, nor an unreasonable ending. The whole parable teaches three things.

First, the kingdom of God is open to all men. This does not sound like a very revolutionary idea. What could be more obvious than the fact that God is no respecter of persons. "There is neither Jew nor Greek, there is neither bond nor free . . . for ye are all one in Christ Jesus" (Gal. 3:28). In theory, at least, most Christians would agree with this proposition. It was a shockingly revolutionary idea to the Jews of Jesus' day. To them the kingdom was open only to the children of Israel or to proselytes from other nations who had accepted the religion of the Jews. Even these were looked upon as second-class citizens of the kingdom of God. We cannot say that the doctrine that all men are equally welcome to God is practiced by all Christians. Yet no one can deny that the Church is one of the most outspoken champions of the idea of human equality today. We can be proud that the first thing Christ taught in this parable is taken seriously by many people.

Jesus taught a second thing in this story. When the wedding feast was opened to everybody, the king came to see what kind of people had come in. Here a new principle enters human history. God does not discriminate between men because of their race, color, economic condition, or social position. There is, however, a divine discrimination that goes deeper than these things. The kingdom of God is open to any man, but every man is under the scrutiny of God. The question God asks is not what a man is outwardly, but what he is inwardly.

Neither society nor the Church has any right to exclude a human being because he is different outwardly. Nevertheless, both share with God the right to expect that a man have a good character and behave decently. The whole fabric of morality, law, and justice rests upon this truth. No man can live just as he pleases. Much is expected of him. The door of God's kingdom stands wide open. Yet God judges who is worthy to enter and remain. Every right that man possesses, spiritual or civil, is equally balanced by an obligation to be a responsible human being. The love of God implies that He also be a judge.

Now we are ready for the third teaching of this parable. The king discovered a guest who did not measure up. "Friend, how camest thou in hither not having a wedding garment?" Jesus is not at all concerned with what the man wore on his back. He is mightily concerned with the fabric of his soul. There are only two qualities that God looks for in a human life. One is sincere repentance. The other is faith. These two woven together form the warp and woof of the acceptable soul. Of course, God would like to find valiant righteousness in a man, but he does not require it for salvation. God would like to see the glowing quality of dauntless courage, but He knows that His children are fearful of many things, so He does not require it. God would like to see in each one of us unceasing charitableness toward our fellow men. But He knows that such charity is beyond our frail capacity. God would like to find us as absolutely obedient to His laws as are the angels. Yet He understands that we fail often to obey. He does not require it. There are many virtues He would like to see in us. The only things He requires are possible to any man. He requires that we be truly sorry for our shortcomings and that we place our ultimate trust in His forgiving love. These make up a suitable wedding garment acceptable to God.

Thus, one of the most difficult parables ever told by Christ illustrates the central truth about man's salvation. Anyone can come to God. Yet he cannot come on his own terms. Each will be judged. But a man will not be judged by his virtues. He will be judged by the genuineness of his sorrow for his failures and by his trust that God's love will never fail.

This parable brings the encouragement of hope to those who know the meaning of despair.

Appendix

Chapters appropriate to particular seasons of the Christian Year:
Advent: 5, 23, 24, 35, 37
Christmastide: 6
Epiphany: 7, 17, 24, 27, 34
Pre-Lent: 2, 9, 32, 36, 38
Lent: 5, 10, 11, 12, 13, 20, 28, 30, 31, 36
Passiontide: 5, 10, 11, 12, 13, 25, 26
Eastertide: 3, 14, 21, 25, 28, 29, 31, 37
Ascensiontide: 16, 17
Whitsuntide: 18, 19, 20, 38
Trinity: 1, 4, 8, 9, 11, 15, 17, 20, 22, 30, 31, 32, 33, 34, 37, 39

Chapters appropriate to following topics:
Holy Baptism: 1, 24
The Sacraments: 5
Church Unity: 21
The Anglican Communion: 5
Thanksgiving: 34